MODEL

Norman Jean Roy

MODEL

THE COMPLETE GUIDE
FOR MEN AND WOMEN

Norman Jean Roy

MARIE ANDERSON BOYD

Foreword by
Norman Jean Roy, Photographer

THUNDER'S
MOUTH
PRESS

Thunder's Mouth Press
632 Broadway
New York
NY 10012

Published in Great Britain by Collins & Brown Ltd., London
First Thunder's Mouth Press Edition 1997

Library of Congress Cataloging-in-Publication Data
Boyd, Marie Anderson, 1958–
Model : the complete guide for men and women / by Marie
Anderson Boyd. -- Rev.
    p.   cm.
    Includes bibliographical references and index.
    ISBN 1-56025-109-3
    1. Models (Persons) -- United States -- Vocational guidance.
    I. Title.
    HD6073.M772U528 1996
    659.1152--do20   96-21211
                     CIP

Distributed by Publishers Group West, 4065 Hollis Street,
Emeryville, CA 94608

Printed in Italy by Grafiche Manfrini - Calliano (TN)

Norman Jean Roy

Dedication

To those who never wavered:
Robert Black
Mary & Joe Boncher
J.F. Cortland Boyd
Jim & Mickey Brdar
Bill Heil
Robert Labate
Stan Malinowski
Bo Medenica
Michael Reed
William Trammell
Suzanne Anderson Vaughn
Eddie Yoshimura
Michael & Deborah de Zonna

To the Aria staff that I continually annoyed with my urgent interruptions on their crazy business days: Andrea, Anna, Brad, Carrie, Chadwick, Chris, Claire, David, Eileen, Kirsten, Kristel, Lilian, Liz, Megan, Miguel, Rod, Sebastian, Terumi, Tony and Yvonne.

To the Aria hair, make-up and clothing artists for their undying commitment.

To Norman Jean Roy for bringing this project to life.

To my unique parents, Marcelle & Bruce Anderson, Jr.

But most of all to God. His continual miracles humble me.

Farewell to Tory Odum and Jeff Crimi – you'll both be missed.

Contents

Norman Jean Roy

CHAPTER 6

MODELING AROUND THE WORLD

CHAPTER 7

ROLES AND TASKS WITHIN THE INDUSTRY

CHAPTER 8

NUTRITION AND EXERCISE

CHAPTER 9

HANDLING YOUR FINANCES

CHAPTER 10

COMMERCIAL ACTING

Carter Smith

INTRODUCTION

As I sit trying to write this, I can't help but reflect back on my amazing, intense career of the past sixteen years. I've included a few details from my résumé for those of you who are not familiar with me. Those who are will perhaps now understand why I'm so driven.

I am thrilled that you're about to read this second edition of my internationally published book. The original draft was written in 1987 while I was working at a major international modeling agency in Chicago. I spent seven years there, beginning as a booker, and was promoted several times until I became vice-president.

After my wonderful experience there I felt it was time to move on to something else. I wasn't sure exactly what the something else was — I just knew that I needed a less corporate environment. (Not that corporate is necessarily a bad thing; in my case the agency had grown so large that I felt lost within its money and power.)

My first solo venture was Model Futures, a model placement and consulting service, which I ran single-handedly for two challenging years. During that time I was continually encouraged to open my own agency, something that I initially resisted because I felt that there were enough agencies in Chicago and that it wasn't a financially wise move. This changed when I developed a client relationship with Mary Boncher, owner of Mary Boncher Model & Talent Management.

We were a perfect match; she had great business and talent management background, and I had thirteen years' experience in the international fashion modeling industry.

Against the advice of many but with the encouragement of a few, we opened Aria Model & Talent Management Ltd in 1992. Within six months we were making money, and since then we've become a multi-million dollar international agency — not bad, considering we went against the advice of so many.

I consider myself to be a late bloomer. My early years were spent believing in everyone else and never in myself. I was insecure and felt I had nothing to offer anyone. At sixteen and 5ft 8in, I tried to become a model, but was turned down because my skin was "too olive" and I was "too tall". In my senior year I was awarded a clothing design scholarship from an out-of-town college. When I told my teacher, she said, "Marie, you'll never be a designer, you don't have any talent." I gave up my scholarship! (At that time I was graduating from high school and was basically homeless and living on food stamps. As desperate as I was, I still didn't reach out against the advice of others to try for myself.)

At seventeen I moved to Chicago with nothing more than my junior high typing class knowledge. Luckily I landed a job working for an employment agency. (To be honest, I think the owner felt sorry for me.) During my three years there, I proved myself to be a valuable employee through hard work and a determination to learn.

Although I was making a comfortable living, those years were a time of agonizing self-exploration. In fact, I felt lost and confused until the photographer Stan Malinowski offered me a job. As soon as I entered his studio, I knew I had found an environment in which I could flourish. I hadn't known that I held skills to organize and execute photo shoots, or that I had the ability to contribute creatively. The self-awakening process was astounding. Stan taught me and allowed me to assume more and more responsibilities as I began to prove myself.

Over a three-year period of working with Stan and traveling internationally, I slowly began to build confidence in myself and my abilities. I learned a great deal and worked very hard. Eventually it was time for another challenge. Stan suggested that I become an agent, and I did. The transition was easy as I had already established myself as an honest, hard-working person within the modeling community.

It was only a few short months after I made the leap into the agency business that I started Cindy Crawford, who was only sixteen at the time. Very few people saw in Cindy what I saw; thankfully she believed in herself enough not to let them discourage her – now she is an

international supermodel and celebrity. Basically this book and my career are testaments to going after your dreams. You wouldn't be reading this second edition of my labour of love had I not defied my father's advice: "Who's going to want to read what you have to say? You don't even have a college degree! You're going nowhere, kid, and you're deceiving yourself in thinking that you'll publish a book."

I proved my father wrong, and you too can confound the doubters. To do this, you must learn your craft and earn the respect of your peers. Being pretty, tall or handsome just isn't enough to become a successful model. You must also have business sense or consult someone who has. Modeling is just like any other business – you must be properly financed in order to compete. I hope this book will prepare you in most areas before pursuing your goal.

Life is definitely a journey, and you make the decision at some point to take control of your path. There's no gain in blaming others or making excuses for not doing something. It is 100 percent up to you, and as long as you know what you want, it can be obtained.

Best of luck!

Marie Anderson Boyd

MARIE ANDERSON BOYD

Bruce Weber

When Marie asked me to be a part of her new book, I was really excited. First of all, it gives me an opportunity to properly acknowledge and thank someone who has been an inspiration to me. Without Marie's guidance, advice, honesty and friendship I would not just have experienced three of the most interesting and rewarding years of my life as a professional model.

Contributing to this book also gives me a chance to share a thought or two with others who are interested in getting involved in modeling. It's a unique world, and because of this, an aspiring model is faced with some unique situations: traveling the world independently, meeting hundreds of interesting people, receiving a lot of attention, making money, living your dream.

These opportunities can bring great rewards and pleasure. An aspiring model should be excited about that, even driven by it. However, someone starting out in this business should also be informed and realistic. For most of us success does not come overnight. There will be a lot of bumps on the road ahead of you and an awful lot of rejections. No one is going to hand you anything. You must be persistent and have faith in yourself to survive this business. It is also important that you do not compromise your values at any time.

Remember that there are no short cuts to real success in life. If you approach the business in a healthy, energetic way, you will enjoy the experiences that lay ahead of you much more.

I hope that your experience as a model is as rewarding for you as it has been for me. I am confident that Marie's book will prove to be very helpful to anyone who is interested in becoming a model, just as her advice and guidance has always been beneficial to me.

MATT KING
Model

I began modeling when I was eleven years old. I thought it was the best job in the world. It seemed easy – all I had to do was sit and smile. As my career progressed, I began to discover all the disadvantages and how demanding the job really was. For example, modeling bathing suits in freezing weather, wearing fur coats in the August heat, or working when you're ill are no fun. My hair becomes badly damaged from all the products and styling it's treated to, and my skin breaks out from make-up applications day after day. I've been accidentally burned with a curling iron, consistently stuck with pins, and pushed and pulled to make the clothes fit properly. This is only the beginning. I can't tell you how much of my own money I have invested in pursuing this career. And only now, after four years, am I beginning to make some of it back.

At first I thought that I was very special and lucky to be a model. I thought there were only a few models around, and only the most beautiful and special girls were chosen by agencies. Wrong! This is a very competitive business, where just about anyone can model and the politics are overwhelming. There are so many different ideas of beauty. In one market they love my look, and in the next they think I'm too exotic.

When I first started modeling, my booker at an international agency made me feel so insecure and ignorant. He spoke down to me and made me feel that if I didn't listen to him that I'd be kicked out of the agency. I didn't stay there long because I knew I wasn't stupid and I did not want to be around someone who made me feel that way.

I discovered very quickly that you must be clear on where you want your career to go. Be a part of the decision-making process in determining how you want to look and what image you want to project. It's a team effort, and it's good to find an agency and booker who will listen to you and be on your side. It is also important to take responsibility for your money. Invest and keep track of it! While I make a nice hourly rate, the agency takes 20 per cent, the I.R.S. takes a piece and there are also expenses such as my composites, international faxes, messengers and so on. By the time I get my check, a lot of money has already been taken out. The business is much less glamorous than it seems.

My advice to young models? Modeling is a strange and difficult lifestyle, and it is not right for everyone. You should really research the industry before you decide to join it. You need to know the pros and cons. If you decide to become a model, you should realize that you'll be constantly moving from city to city, which makes it hard to keep friends and maintain relationships. You need someone in the business that you can trust and talk to. I was lucky to find Marie. She's the one person that I trust in this crazy business!

Good luck.

ASHLI DEGENFORD
Model

GIRL & CO.

LEI & LUI
Fare sesso può essere difficile, ma....

MODA
UN LOOK SENZA MANICHE

VACANZE IN FRANCIA
Proposte, occasioni sconti e consigli pratici

LOVE SPECIAL
Tutti i segreti del petting

NERI PER CASO
E' UN'ALTRA MUSICA

Winston

FOREWORD

Fashion is everywhere. From campaign ads to catalogues, from magazines to charity benefits, fashion has become such a part of our society that it can single-handedly shape and define our attitudes and perceptions towards life and the world around us.

Until just a few years ago, modeling was perceived more as a way to make a living rather than the avenue to super stardom that it has become. With models becoming household names, it is very difficult to overlook their importance in the overall production and direction taken by designers and magazines in producing ad campaigns and editorial stories.

Since modeling requires more than just a pretty face, Marie Anderson Boyd's *Model* provides a tremendous training aid which new models can use to solidify their abilities and knowledge about the industry on both personal and professional levels. I highly recommend this book to anyone considering a career in the modeling industry.

NORMAN JEAN ROY
Photographer

How to Get an Agency

Agents are constantly on the lookout for new models, and have been known to pluck potential talent out of the crowd. More frequently, though, it takes hard work and dedication to become a successful model.

One of the key components in a successful modeling career is proper financing. Usually, the burden of providing it falls on parents, but regardless of where the money comes from, when you become a model you become an independent contractor, which makes you self-employed. Being self-employed makes you the owner of your own company. Chapter 9 goes into greater detail on the subject of money and the management of your new company.

Right now, before you begin your career in modeling, you must consider the financial outlay you will have to make and take steps to ensure that you spend wisely.

INITIAL EXPENDITURES

The ideal situation is to spend very little money before finding an agency to represent you. However, impatience and rapid communications probably mean that you already have. Whether you've spent money on a modeling school, photographer or whatever, you will still end up spending more money once you're represented by a legitimate agency. Your agent is responsible for guiding you towards wise investments, which will vary according to where you live, what year it is and what you've accomplished prior to arriving at the agency.

INITIAL OUTLAY ($ APPROXIMATE)

Portfolio photo shoots (to start)	1000	(F)
	600	(M)
Main book, lasers and prints	250	
Agency laser book (12 shots)	48	
Composite: 1000 b & w hard	300	
or 100 color laser	225	
Headsheet	175	
Agency promotional book	500	
Model's bag (see pages 45 & 47)	2500	(F)
	600	(M)
Make-up	800	(F)
	40	(M)
Passport	50	

Total: $5548 color comp or $5623 b/w (F)
        $2488 color comp or $2563 b/w (M)

If models want to have pictures shot before they go see agencies, they should make them natural: use Elle magazine as a guide.

PETER McCLAFFERTY Agent

FINDING YOUR NICHE

There are several types of modeling agency representing various model types. Each agency has an image it tries to project and maintain. Every model represented by the agency is an extension of its image. What is your image? What kind of model could you be?

WOMEN:
Are you 5ft 8in or taller?
Do you weigh 110–120 lb?
Do you measure 34B–24–34?
Do you wear a size 6–8?

MEN:
Are you 5ft 11in–6ft 1in tall?
Do you weigh 155–180 lb?
Do you measure 40–32–38?
Do you wear a size 40R?

Do you resemble any of the models in the fashion magazines?
Do you have clear, evenly toned skin?
Do you have even, white teeth?

If you have answered yes to several of these questions, then perhaps you could become a print fashion and/or runway model.

If you are shorter and heavier than a straight size model, you may fit into a more specialized market, such as full-figure modeling. (This category does not yet exist for male models. For further information on male modeling, please see Chapter 5.)

Do you have beautiful hands, feet or legs? If so, perhaps you could become a part model.

This chapter concentrates on print fashion modeling (known as photographic modeling in the U.K.).

▼ *The letter you enclose with your snapshots should be brief and to the point, like the one shown below. First impressions are important, so make sure it is either typed neatly on white paper, or beautifully handwritten on attractive stationery, and be sure to include a stamped, self-addressed envelope for a response.*

Tel: (555) 123 4567

999 City Road
Bigtown
E. Maryland

March 23rd, 19…

Dear New Faces

My name is Jane Smith. I am 5ft 8 inches tall, weigh 110 lb, and have blonde hair and blue eyes.

I am interested in becoming a model and hope you will like the snapshots I am enclosing. If you are interested in interviewing me, I am available after 3 P.M. daily.

Yours sincerely

Jane Smith

Jane Smith

▲ ▶ *Agents are happy to arrange an initial interview based on reasonable snapshots. Make sure you include one full-face and one full-length (preferably in a swimsuit).*

I have signed quite a few models who have sent pictures through the mail. All they need to submit is a head shot and a body shot. Keep it very simple – minimal make-up and simply styled hair.

LEAH McCLOSKEY Agent

BEFORE THE INTERVIEW

Before you interview with an agent or agencies there are a few critical factors to keep in mind. Very few people are aware of these points as they are not discussed openly within the modeling business.

I've always thought it odd that doctors and lawyers must be educated in order to counsel us, but agents, who give out advice all the time, require no formal qualifications. When something goes wrong, it's not unusual to hear of doctors and lawyers being sued for malpractice, but I've never yet heard of an agent being sued for mismanaging a model's career. Apart from civil laws, there is nothing to protect aspiring models from ill-informed agents.

Requirements to become an agent vary from place to place. In the state of Illinois in the US, for example, the requirements are minimal. You must have no criminal record, be able to read English, study a pamphlet on employment rules and regulations, go to the Department of Labor with fifty dollars, take a test (based upon a career that has nothing to do with being an agent) and if you pass you're now licenced to practice. That's it!

The situation is much the same elsewhere in the world. Anyone can set up a modeling agency without knowing a thing about the business. For this reason, if no other, you must be very careful who you place your trust in. It's natural to assume that the agent is experienced and has your best interests in mind but, unfortunately, this isn't always the case. There are tons of inexperienced agents around who have gotten there by being married to someone influential, or by having a brother or sister working in the business, or by stepping into the breach when a booker suddenly left and remaining there, despite having no proper training. Some have the best of intentions, but their lack of accurate knowledge often misleads the trusting new model.

Don't be naive and think that you're immune to all these goings-on. They are rampant throughout the world, regardless of which prestigious name is on the door. It's your job to research things thoroughly and ask lots of questions to determine someone's experience. Talk to models who are represented by your chosen agencies, and not necessarily to those whose names are given to you. Be creative and you can find out exactly what you need to know. But at the end of the day it's vital that you follow your instincts and make the best decision you can at the time.

Leave the boyfriends at home!
GERARD BISIGNANO Agent

GETTING AN INTERVIEW

As all agencies do not represent all ages and sizes, it is imperative to know which agency to see and why. You could begin by going through the telephone book and calling all the modelling agencies listed, or asking other models and photographers for referrals.

Be prepared for brisk treatment when calling an agency. Remember the receptionist has to deal with hundreds of calls from clients, agents, photographers, models, messengers and hopefuls all needing immediate attention. If the receptionist sounds abrupt, do not take it personally. You can always ask the best time to call back so your questions can be answered more fully. An initial telephone inquiry might go as follows:

RECEPTIONIST: Good morning, Aria Model and Talent, may I help you?
CALLER: Yes, I am interested in becoming a model. How can I arrange an interview with your agency?
RECEPTIONIST: (Will give a short explanation)
    or
RECEPTIONIST: Good morning, Aria.
CALLER: Good morning. I'm a new model and I'd like to arrange an interview with your agency.
RECEPTIONIST: (Will give a short explanation)

Each agency has its own system of appointments. When you call, the receptionist will inform you if a personal interview can be arranged, or tell you where to send your photos. Sometimes agencies have open auditions (walk-in interviews) and the receptionist will tell you where and when to attend. Be prepared for the receptionist to decide if you are suitable for the agency and if you may see an agent. (Note that it is very unprofessional to turn up unannounced at an agency and expect an interview without an appointment.)

I have signed many models who have simply sent me decent snapshots. Mail your pictures or a composite with a stamped self-addressed envelope and write your name and telephone number on the back of each shot. Send whatever you can afford not to have returned. Agencies get bogged down with mail and it is very difficult to keep track of every single photo submitted. If a friend takes your photos, make sure the photos look like you. Your make-up should look very clean and your natural hairstyle should be shown; do not curl, spray or back-comb. Be sure to include a bathing suit shot to show the proportions of your body.

If an agency is interested in interviewing you, it will contact you by phone or mail. This could take a few weeks, so be prepared to wait.

THE INTERVIEW

It is not necessary to have a portfolio of photographs to obtain an interview. Agencies are used to making initial assessments from snapshots. A good agent can assess your marketability from looking at you in person and will tell you candidly if she can help you to pursue a career in modeling, or if you should see other agencies. (Note that agents can be male or female. For the purposes of this book, I refer to the agent as "she" throughout.) Make the most of your interview by remembering the following points.

- Being interviewed as a model is just like being interviewed for any other job; you have to sell yourself.

- Wear clean, casual clothes, choosing fitted rather than loose garments.

- Use minimal make-up and keep your hair clean and simply styled.

- Have your hands manicured. It's fine not to wear polish, but be sure your nails are clean, filed and buffed.

- Bring whatever recent flattering pictures you may have.

- Bring paper and pen and be prepared to write down any instructions or referrals that the agent might give you. (It's so irritating when an interviewee says, "Oh, will you write that down for me?" You are seeking free advice and possibly acquiring a new agency, so don't start off on the wrong foot. The agent is not your secretary.)

- Be on time. Call if you are going to be late.

- Be patient if the agent is delayed. Other business, such as photographers calling, models needing help, or unexpected emergencies, must take priority. Agents first take care of the talent they represent and then go on to considering others. Your interview is a brief interlude in a busy day, so make your interruption a pleasant one.

- When you meet the agent you should look into her eyes, smile and, if you wish, give a firm handshake.

You need to look clean, fresh and neat for an interview. ▶
Choose fitted clothes that match the image you want to project, and choose an agency that already projects your sort of image.

- When you sit down with the agent, wait for her to ask for your pictures, if you have them. Do not assume that she will want to have them thrust at her immediately. When requested, place your portfolio in the correct direction for the agent's view.

- Do not inspect or fidget with anything on the agent's desk unless you are invited to do so. Consider anything that does not belong to you or that is not handed to you to be private property – no trespassing!

- If the agent should leave the desk, do not get up and walk around – it is presumptuous to assume you have free access to the environment. Sit patiently and wait for the agent to return.

One of the first questions I ask an aspiring model is, "What do you want to accomplish from this interview with me today?"

I've heard, "I don't know what I'm doing here. I mean, you're the agent, don't you tell me?"

I've also heard, "I've been interested in becoming a fashion model for a few years and now have the money and time to try it. I also understand that Aria is the best in fashion modelling and I want to start at the top. Could you please give me the advice and direction I need?"

I became irritated with the first interviewee because she was wasting my valuable time. I was delighted with the second because she knew which agency was respected in her field and she stated her reason for being there very clearly.

Terrible haircuts, excess weight, bad skin, poor attitudes and unprofessional behaviour can turn an agent off immediately. Personality is a major part in deciding if I'll sign a model. I assume that you will interact with clients in the same manner that you interact with me. I believe that if a model does not already know how to communicate, then it will take too long to teach her or him. I have signed many models who may not have a look that I immediately believe in, but they have sold me on their motivation and personality.

Always ask questions. You must realize that you are interviewing the agent just as the agent is interviewing you. If the interviewer is not going to be your agent once you have signed up, find out who will be. You have to like and trust that person. Be very careful. You and your agent should agree on your

I hate when models come to an interview with their hair all foo-fooed out with more mousse than you can drown a rat in or with so much make-up that you can't see what they look like.

GERARD BISIGNANO Agent

career strategy. Here are some questions that may help you in your interview:

- How would you market me?
- How much money will I have to invest immediately and in the long term?
- Do you feel I will get work quickly?
- Do I require any immediate physical changes, such as a haircut, weight loss, skin treatment or cosmetic dentistry?
- How much commission do you take?
- When and how do I get paid?
- What is/will be my hourly rate?

Remember, just because a specific agency is considered to be the best for other people does not mean that it is necessarily the best agency for you. I have actually had aspiring models argue with me that Aria is the best agency for them and they insist that I am making a mistake in not representing them. My response is, "Why would you want to be represented by an agency which does not want to represent you?" It is imperative that both the model and the agency believe in the product, understand how to market the product and agree to work together.

Over the years I have signed on quite a few models whom I have initially turned down – sometimes even twice. Timing is very important. At the time that you happen to be interviewing with an agency, it might already have a couple of models whom you resemble. The agency will protect the talent that it already has under contract and thus avoid internal competition within the same market at the same time.

If you are really determined to become a model, you won't allow a few rejections to discourage you, even if you have been rejected by every agency in your market. Think about it – why were you rejected? Did you receive any constructive criticism you could put into practice before trying again? Perhaps you need to lose

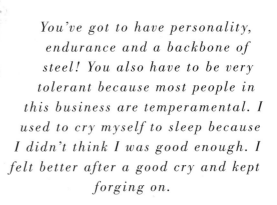

You've got to have personality, endurance and a backbone of steel! You also have to be very tolerant because most people in this business are temperamental. I used to cry myself to sleep because I didn't think I was good enough. I felt better after a good cry and kept forging on.

VANESSA VICTOR Model

weight, clear up bad skin or grow out an awful haircut? As I have mentioned before, an agency can always provide reasons for rejecting someone. Many aspiring models make heartfelt promises to me, swearing that if I sign them with the agency, they will take care of any immediate problem. I rarely listen to their promises. There are just too many other dedicated people out there for me to bet on those who haven't got their act together when they arrive for interview. I say this so you'll understand why some agents may reject you, not to scare you away from trying. You can't possibly know how each agent will respond.

Large agency, small agency, exclusive, non-exclusive, multiply listed (being represented by more than one agency) – are all controversial topics. I cannot tell which is best for you. Just do lots of research, ask lots of questions (keeping notes), observe the agencies as you are interviewing to see how they operate, then follow your instincts.

It is possible that you might make a mistake. The important thing is that you make a decision on something and take a step forward. You will continually learn if you make decisions. You are the one who must begin to take control of your new business – *you*.

I'm always on the lookout for some special quality that makes a great face and body outstanding. Personality, style and self-confidence should shine through. If there is an element of that special quality, a good agent will develop and sell it. Once the model starts to feel that momentum, then the rush is on.

HUGGY RAGNARSSON Freelance Scout

Norman Jean Roy

When You Have an Agency

A modeling agency can often seem like a chaotic environment to the uninitiated, but beneath the frenzy a lot of hard work is going on.

Congratulations! You've got yourself an agency and you're raring to go. At the risk of sounding like a wet blanket, I'm now going to give you a few words of caution.

Modeling is a tough business, and however sensible you are, you're bound to take some knocks. My mother always used to tell me, "When you've lost your sense of humor you've lost everything." Those words of wisdom have brought me through many difficult times as I've grown up in the fashion world. You have to maintain a great sense of humor to endure some of the nonsense that will inevitably come your way. If you laugh it off, you will come through with flying colors. I tease many new interviewees that I wouldn't wish this business on anyone.

For now be warned that your life will be turned upside-down. If you are clever and keep your wits about you, you'll adjust very quickly and, hopefully, with minimal pain. It is not being cynical to say that there are nasty people in this industry – there are nasty ones outside it too. There are bound to be times when you will experience problems with such people generally.

Like professional athletes, models are given a talent, only in this case it's a beautiful face and body. If you use them as a means to an end, you can create a terrific career for yourself.

MARJORIE GRAHAM Agent

THE SECRET OF SUCCESS

This can be quickly summed up in two words:

SACRIFICE – to give up something in the short term for the sake of something better in the long term; and COMPETE – to strive for an objective.

Both these words indicate a single-mindedness which you must have to survive as a model – and sometimes they can make your life very difficult.

A model is constantly concerned with such things as diet, exercise, sleep, skin care, make-up, hair, clothes, and T.V. commercials. You'll become immersed in a whole new world which you have to juggle simultaneously with your existing lifestyle. There will be endless and inevitable changes. Modeling is a very self-centered career and your family and friends may be slow to realize that your time with them will necessarily be curtailed. They'll watch you spending a lot of money that most likely won't produce an immediate return. They'll see a physical change in you as you become

more educated about how to present yourself. They'll see an emotional change as you become more confident. I've seen models suffer tremendously because of concerned parents, jealous girlfriends and intimidated boyfriends. It takes strength of character to consider yourself and your career constantly without hurting those around you. Keeping your family and close friends abreast of your daily activities can aid the transition; this way they'll understand your involvement with some of your other concerns.

People sometimes have funny ideas about the modeling business, seeing it as one long, self-indulgent ego trip. However misconceived these ideas, they can threaten your relationships, so you'd better be prepared to decide what your sacrifices will be. It's not uncommon for models to become selfish and neurotic, but it's up to you if you let yourself succumb to the negative aspects of the business.

What does it mean to "compete" as a model? One parallel that may help you understand the "competition" is the idea of an Olympic hopeful going after a gold medal in swimming. That swimmer spends hours training every day, as well as juggling other obligations. He or she will practice form and speed and not be distracted by developing dry skin and discolored, brittle hair, by smelling of chlorine, by missing out on social activities with family and friends, or by worrying about other swimmers who may have more experience and talent. All these things count for nothing if you have a goal you really want to achieve.

The same single-mindedness applies to modeling. Thousands of people have preceded you in your chosen career. Many have been downright vicious and inconsiderate in reaching their goal, but you don't have to be like that; indeed, you'll get a lot further if you're not! It's always better to make friends rather than enemies.

I found a new model at a convention. The agency paid for her air fare to come to Chicago and we also paid for a hotel room for her and her father for one week. We allowed her to stay rent-free in the models' apartment. She broke the no-pets rule by getting a cat and then lied about how it got into the apartment. We advanced her money for portfolio photographs and her composite. When she became ill late one Sunday night, our booker drove her to the hospital and spent the night with her because she was scared. She then returned to her home town to recuperate from her illness. We expected her to return in two weeks. Well, she returned all right! One evening I just happened to see her walking down the street arm in arm with a friend. I learned the next day that she was on an audition in Chicago through another agency. She never had the courtesy to tell us she was dissatisfied with our representation. She told people that she didn't think we believed in her look. (Well, if we didn't prove it by our attentions, what else could we have done?)

We wasted a lot of time and money because of this model, but this story is typical of many and there are hundreds more that every agent can cite. It's up to you to break the mold that this over-saturated industry has produced. If you're new and have no track record, don't take it personally if people don't bend over backwards to help you — it's because too many nasty people have tainted their enthusiasm for assisting unknown, aspiring models.

In promoting yourself (competing), people will inevitably misunderstand you and take your confidence for arrogance. What is wrong with believing in yourself? Nothing! But you must keep it all in perspective. I amaze people when I tell them that I am an excellent agent. I am! I can't balance my checking acount, I don't know how to change a tire on a car; in fact, there are lots of things I can't do, but agenting is what I do know. And I know it well! Would you want to work with an agent who didn't believe in herself? Or who couldn't make a decision or protect you and your career? How confident would you be in her representation if she were sheepish and always avoiding issues? (Recently I met up with an old high school chum, Eric and his friend. After I began updating Eric on my progress over the years, he turned to his friend and said, "Marie's not conceited, she's just convinced!" I was amused at his reaction. What do people want to hear — that I'm doing poorly and I'm not going anywhere in life? They'll never hear it from my mouth!)

The kids think of rejection as a personal attack on their physical appearance, when in reality they didn't get the jobs because they just weren't right for them... Once they establish in their own minds that they are good-looking and accept that rejection isn't a personal attack, they make it a lot easier on themselves.

PAUL DAVID FISHER   Agent

You will have to work hard at establishing yourself as a competitive, considerate, confident, worthwhile product. When people tease you or question you, just laugh them off. My father, who was a chemical engineer on the Apollo moon project, had no understanding of the fashion industry and always insisted that I didn't have a real job. He maintained that until I got a college degree I wouldn't become successful. People outside this industry have a distorted perception of what really goes on. I know that this can be a frustrating, expensive, depressing, degrading career — on the other hand, it can be educational, lucrative, uplifting, and confidence-building. In order to become successful you have to maintain your own ethics and morals. Remain true to yourself, take care of yourself and the people around you, and always be professional.

Because modeling is such a selfish profession and each job can be your last, you try and learn from each job — you try and move forward — and you do tend to focus all of what you are learning into yourself. It takes a special kind of person to be able to live with not knowing where the next pay check is coming from, to accept the responsibility of never working again, and still feel very positive about yourself. Certain things, such as going to the movies with friends, become inconsequential next to working out, having a make-up lesson, or going to a testing.

ANDI WESTERMAN
Photographer's Representative

GETTING TO KNOW YOUR PROFESSION

A model is a product, just like any other product being sold. The main difference is that the model is a human being, and as such is capable of emotions which can sometimes interfere with the sale. It is crucial that you understand the industry in order to learn how to separate the emotional part of yourself from the product part. I have a simple analogy that might lend insight to this difficult process.

Do you brush your teeth? What brand of toothpaste do you use? How long have you been using that brand? Chances are you have either used the same brand for years or you change brands very quickly. Similarly, photographers and clients might use the same models for years or they might change very quickly.

It is very difficult to know what each client's habits are and how to handle them, so be consistent in your behaviour and approach each meeting with the intention of selling the product. Modeling is a business, just like any other. The glamour and excitement of the business does not mean that you should be any less professional in your approach.

How did you hear about your particular brand(s) of toothpaste? Word of mouth, television commercials, magazine advertisements, billboards? All these sources and more are called advertising. No matter what the source, if the product is being talked about or seen, it's being advertised. It is imperative that you advertise your product, too. You advertise yourself through word of mouth, through photographers, make-up artists, hairdressers and stylists, through your portfolio and composite, and through your print bookings (published photographs). These are all components of your advertising campaign. A modeling agency acts as your advertising agency and it is essential to have one before going any further. You should not spend any money on your advertising campaign until you have a strategy determining how you will design, package, and advertise yourself. It is the agent's responsibility to assess the product (you) and to speculate on your marketability in their market and others. Such assessments are based upon years of experience in working with models and clients, and traveling around the world doing research.

The message you send is not always the message received, so you have to communicate carefully – check who your audience is and how you're projecting yourself. In part, we know who we are based upon feedback from other people. It works in a loop. We have to project an image. People respond to us based upon what they see – perhaps it's confidence, the way we dress, or the way we walk. Our own self-concept develops from other people's reactions to us.

DONNA SURGES-TATUM
Ph.D

The market is the most important factor in a successful career. A model could make a lot of money shooting catalogue in Hamburg, Germany, then go to New York and possibly never work in catalogue. To be successful, you must place your product in the market(s) most likely to purchase you. (Chances are that you won't sell many African-American hair products in a predominantly white neighborhood store and vice-versa. The strategy would be to sell minority products in areas where the minorities live.) Be sure to do your research before going into any market; the ways of doing this are more fully described on page 28.

I'm very conscious of my appearance – to me it's all part of the business. It's packaging – just like any other product. The tip I'd give to new models is that personality and how you present yourself are the basis of how the client will interact with you.

MICHAEL RAMION Model

REPUTATION

Do you know people who, no matter what they say they'll do, just never do it? Even as they are saying the words, you are sure they'll never follow through, so eventually you never take them seriously. Can you honestly claim you are not one of these people? Do you always do what you say you are going to do?

Do you know people who, no matter when you speak to them, are always unhappy and have a negative attitude? They just never have anything pleasant or nice to say? It's so depressing that you may even want to go in another direction when you see them coming! Do you come across in a negative way?

You must realize that there are hundreds of kids who can do the same job as you. The clients want something a little more special than someone to fill the job. They are looking for a personality and attitude of professionalism that they can work with. Everyone wants to have a pleasant day; make the clients' job easy so they can leave the shoot smiling.

ALLAN BOYD Model

Do you know people who, no matter when you speak to them, are always happy and have a positive attitude? Do they always have something nice to say and uplift you no matter what your mood? You'll probably even go out of your way just to say hello to such people if they're coming in your direction! Do you come across in a positive way?

The thoughts people have about you could be considered your reputation. All products have reputations, and a model's is closely linked to attitude;

▶ *Whether you're new to the modeling business, or an old hand, it's important to keep up with trends in fashion photography. The best way to do this is to subscribe to a wide variety of magazines.*

Norman Jean Roy

sometimes they are bad and sometimes they are good. Be sure you develop an enthusiastic, dependable, positive reputation early in your career. That reputation will follow you throughout life.

Imagine yourself as a tube of toothpaste on a store shelf. You have to design your package to compete against other brands, both established and new. What makes your product so special and different? Why should the customer select your product instead of another one? What do you have to offer that someone else does not? Yes, this may sound silly, but if you now understand the parallel, you have come a long way in understanding your profession and making your career more successful.

The secret of success is not simply being beautiful – attitude, initiative, determination, and a fun personality are other important elements.

CELA WISE Model and Actress

GETTING TO KNOW YOUR MARKET

The market is the city and the type of clients there. If you are just beginning your career as a model, you may not know a lot about your market. All the more reason to research your city well. If you're planning on going into a new market or city, you must ask lots of questions and read as much about that area as you can. Ask where the work is, where you fit in and what percentage of the market your "look" fills. If there is not a high demand for you, you might consider moving to another market. Chapters 5 and 6 discuss the different "looks" and markets more extensively.

Your agent could well be your main source of reference, but do phrase your questions precisely or you may get misleading answers. For example, some agents rarely travel outside the country in which they operate, so they do not know the way a foreign market operates. However, this might not deter them from giving you fifth-hand information which could be riddled with inaccuracies.

To avoid this sort of problem, always ask direct questions, such as: Have you been to Milan? What sort of look do they like? And make sure you get direct answers. If in any doubt, ask fellow models who have done what you want to do for the benefit of their experience. Telephone agencies in the particular market you're going to and ask for their advice (some provide fact sheets). Note that agencies throughout the world speak English and most will be happy to pass on a few

local hints. For general information about foreign markets (climate, customs and so on), contact the country's tourist office for free literature. At the very least, visit your local reference library. If you end up in a totally alien environment, like Japan, you'll be thankful to have done your research thoroughly.

Over the years I have seen many models improperly marketed. As a result, I have learned daily lessons on how to prevent the models I deal with from making the same mistakes. The secret is to develop your own understanding of the market and to realize the importance of marketing yourself within the market you wish to work. A good professional model can work in just about any market. However, as a new model it would be wise for you to start your career in a market with a high demand for your look. Remember: each time you change markets your agent will change your portfolio and composite.

Don't arrive unannounced. Have your agency contact another agency in the city that you wish to visit. Be sure to send comps in advance so that they can promote you before you arrive. Your agency can do the groundwork by calling for you in advance to inquire about the market, but then it's your task to get out and see the clients once you arrive.

PAUL WADINA Model

PORTFOLIO ASSEMBLY

We have already established that your portfolio is one of the key components of your advertising campaign. Now you need to know how to put it together. Every agent will address this area differently. However, I am sure that we would all agree that the photos inside your book should be only the best that you can provide at that time in your career. I have interviewed thousands of models over the years, many of whom believe that any photo is better than none. I disagree totally! Remember, you are competing with thousands of models around the world, so you should only show photos that make you look terrific. Note, too, that it is a mistake to show contact sheets, as you probably do not look perfect in every shot.

It does not matter whether you have more black and white photos than color; great pictures are great pictures, regardless of their color. Some agents might suggest that you shoot more black and white than color because it is less expensive. (In the U.K. agents always want to see some black and white photos in a portfolio, even when the model is experienced.) Some companies in large markets can print color quickly and cheaply. You can send your slides to them by courier and have your color prints returned in a few days. Again, you should rely on your agency for proper direction in all these areas.

I feel that your portfolio should "read" just like any other book: it should have a terrific beginning, a strong middle and a sensational ending. Remember, you should have people wanting to turn the pages with curiosity. Each page should satisfy that curiosity. It should display your strengths to potential clients and show what you are capable of selling, be it clothes, cars, or cosmetics.

In the beginning it is very difficult to provide each client with photos they can identify with. Don't get frustrated – it will all come in good time. I have already mentioned the importance of patience. If you don't have any now, you'd better find some. The development of a portfolio can be a very expensive, long, and arduous process, but well worth it.

The types of photo you should shoot depend on what you have to sell and your market. (Some experienced models will have different looks for different markets.) In the early days heed your agent's advice and use your common sense. If you have a great body, perhaps you'll shoot a lot of body shots. If you have excellent skin and hair, shoot a lot of beauty shots. If your legs are terrific, shoot a few leg shots. The idea is to advertise what you have to offer the clients, concentrating on your best features. If your body is not that competitive yet, do not shoot body shots. If your skin and hair are not in excellent condition, you'd better start getting them there; do not shoot beauty shots until you are ready!

It is very important to be versatile. However, do not be so extreme and inconsistent that you confuse the client. Models often show themselves so completely differently that a client cannot get a fix on how they will look for their photo session. You must always show yourself in a relatively similar way. Until you are experienced and really understand yourself my best advice is to keep things straightforward – the make-up and hair, soft; lighting, simple; the clothes and mood, uncomplicated.

The total number of photos that you should use from each photo session depends primarily on the art direction. For an editorial spread, you might use as many as five photos, say, one large and four small. The large one could be displayed on one side of the spread and the four smaller photos opposite. If you have only one terrific photo, I would prefer to see it alone rather than displayed with a photo that clashes. For example, it would be a mistake to display a bathing suit shot next to a fur coat.

A PORTFOLIO SHOULD TELL A STORY WHICH HOLDS THE VIEWER'S INTEREST FROM BEGINNING TO END.

Regan Cameron

1   The opening page should be bold, showing a shot of the model looking terrific. This is often the main shot used on the comp-card.

Stewart Shining

2   Focusing on the body and legs, this spread shows that the model is suitable for lingerie and part modeling.

Stewart Shining

3   These editorial pages show the proportions of the model's body and that she has beautiful hair.

Guzman

4 Soft and young studio shots show that the model is in good shape.

7 More sophisticated studio shots show the model's versatility.

Ellen Von Unwerth

Regan Cameron

5 Exterior shots show the model working on location and displaying lots of animation.

8 The more tailored clothing in these shots show that the model can work in different markets.

Stewart Shining

Ellen Von Unwerth

6 Humor and personality are revealed in these shots of the model wearing light, casual clothing.

9 The final page in the portfolio has a more dramatic look, a great contrast to the model's earlier young and soft look.

Winston

1   The opening page of this portfolio has a
     striking photo of twin models.

Robert Jaso · Blair Kruse

2   These swimwear shots show the models' physique.

Robert Jaso

3   More body shots, but these show more of the
     faces and skin quality.

Robert Jaso

4   Clean, fresh headshots.

Paul Rackley

5   Studio shots, showing casual clothing and sleepwear.

Scott Teitler

6   These shots of light winter clothes follow on well
     from the previous body shots.

Pedro Spoggi · Drew Riker

7   Casual and moody location shots, showing the
     full body.

Pedro Spoggi · Donald MacPherson

8   Moody head shots, showing strong features and good skin.

Peter Ho · Aldo Fallai

9   The portfolio closes with sophisticated editorial
     images – a complete contrast to the lively opening shot.

If possible, also try to include photos of you interacting with other models. This will show catalogue clients that you can work with others in a compatible way. However, do not include such a photo if you are not looking your best. If another model is the focus of the photo, your agent will decide if it is wise to show you next to competition.

At the beginning of your fashion modeling career your portfolio should include:

- At least two head shots with two different expressions (one smiling and one serious, or one in the studio and one outdoors).

- At least two fashion shots (one casual and one a little more formal). If you move well, you might like to include an action shot.

- At least one full-length shot showing the proportions of your body (feet to knees, knees to thighs, thighs to waist, waist to shoulders, shoulders to the top of your head). You could wear a bathing suit, leotard or lingerie, depending on what makes you comfortable and what is the most flattering to your figure.

▲ *If you have a particular skill, such as swimming, horseback-riding, surfing, track, or gymnastics, it is a good idea to include a shot of you in action.*

I have a pattern that I normally follow when I arrange a portfolio. I begin with fall/winter and go into spring/summer seasons if I'm arranging the book during colder months, and vice versa if I'm doing it during warmer weather. This means that models either start with lots of clothes on and slowly take them off, or start in bathing suits and lingerie and slowly add more clothes until wearing heavy sweaters and coats. You can also include photos of yourself participating in sports or other activities towards the end. You may be an equestrian, so include a photo of you riding. If you are a good skier, include a photo of you on the slopes. If you have a nice photo of you on the catwalk, include that too. The idea is to advertise what you have to sell. If your portfolio doesn't win you one job, it may open up a conversation that could eventually lead you into another one.

PORTFOLIO SIZE

The actual model portfolio size is generally around 9 x 12^1/$_2$ inches. It varies slightly from agency to agency, depending upon the manufacturer. Most modeling agencies have their company name and/or logo printed on the front or back of the portfolio. You don't have to have one with your agency logo on it, but it really helps. It quickly tells anyone reviewing your portfolio which agency you're with, and to be honest, it's also a status symbol to have a top agency logo on the front of your portfolio. Models carry them proudly as they hand them to people for inspection. And don't worry if you switch agencies. Most have their logo available in sticker form to cover any former agency name. If not, they'll suggest that you buy one of their portfolios.

Most agencies charge for portfolios, but some don't. Never assume anything, always ask. In a hectic agency someone could easily forget to explain that you're paying for it (eventually). And it could end up being deducted by the agency from the money you've earned through them. Portfolios generally cost around $45.

Various styles of portfolio are available. I suggest you choose one that opens just like any other book: zippers and handles are cumbersome and outdated. Whatever style you opt for, do remember that your portfolio is a critical sales tool to lure in potential clients. Please do not use it as a holdall. It should carry only unscratched plastic pages enclosing your prints and just a few cards in the back. Don't include your friends' comp collection, family snapshots, laundry lists, or other paraphernalia – it's a sales presentation. Let the client see your beautiful photos and how nicely you move in the clothing. Show it proudly!

Contemporary portfolios are smaller, lighter, and neater than previously because they no longer have zippers or bulky handles.

MINI-BOOKS VS. LASER BOOKS

Back in the 1980s it was common practice for models to have mini-books, which were smaller versions of their big book. Now, in the 1990s, they have pretty much been replaced by laser books which contain high-quality (laser) photocopies rather than real photographs. (In the U.K. some agents prefer to use Konica prints because the quality is more reliable, but they are much more expensive.)

Laser books are generally the same size as your main portfolio (see page 33) and it is extremely useful to have several copies. First of all you need a back-up in case your main book is lost or stolen, and then you need copies for all the agencies that represent you at home and overseas. This allows them to promote you while you're not available to meet the client in person with your main book.

Laser prints of your photos must be trimmed to fit into your portfolio. The laser-print portfolio is then arranged by the agency that you send it to. As each market varies and each agent has her own idea of how to market you in her city, it's much easier to go to a laser service and order several same-size laser copies which can fit into any international model portfolio and be sent to any agency in any country.

Laser copies of your portfolio contents offer many advantages. The main one is that high-quality reproductions of original photographs, tear sheets, or slides can be made, usually in minutes. High-quality prints, on the other hand, generally take about two days.

Be warned, however, that laser proofs are only as good as the machine operator. I've seen some awful-looking copies, mainly due to poorly trained laser operators. Your objective is to have excellent copies at a low price. If you don't feel the copies you've been offered are excellent, give them back and ask for the manager. If the manager cannot improve the quality to your satisfaction, take your business elsewhere.

Some companies specialize in making laser copies for models, producing portfolios, as well as model composites (I'll cover that in the composite area). I prefer these specialist companies as they offer quality and a quick turn-round. They have highly trained staff

who understand the need for top-notch reproduction, with natural skin tones, accurate colors, and perfect focus.

A model recently came to me with laser copies in which her skin looked green, although the original photo had not been shot that way. The laser operator obviously thought he was being creative, but modeling clients need to see accurate flesh tones, especially if you're of Mediterranean, African, or Asian descent.

Some companies offer laminating services for laser prints. This is very helpful for more established models or for warm climates, as over a period of time, lasers often stick to the inside of the plastic page in your portfolio. A model I know wanted to save money, so he sent his unlaminated laser prints by courier from Miami to Chicago. By the time they arrived they were all stuck together, so we had to start all over again. The moral is that lamination is an insurance policy, but I generally recommend it only for the professional. New models change their books so often that it's really not necessary.

If you are still using mini-books, please don't throw them out; I don't want to get into trouble with your existing agent. I do occasionally still see them being used in smaller markets, and I must admit that some established models still use them. My comments about mini-books merely reflect the current trend. I suggest you continue using them until it's obvious that you have to change.

If you make five laser copies of your main book, it will cost about $300, as most laser prints cost around $3 each. Expensive, isn't it? Just another example of how your modeling career expenses add up. Nevertheless, laser prints are much cheaper than conventional photographs.

Now that I've dealt with laser books, it's time to mention computers. When I update this book again, I'll probably be talking about CD-ROMs. In fact, if computer designers had their way, we'd eliminate mini-books, laser books, main books, and composites, and just buy their software so everyone could be put on computer disk. This possibility is extremely current and very controversial. For now, just concentrate on making laser copies.

Model photo by Neal Barr for Matrix

*Mini-books have become largely unnecessary because
agencies can now produce inexpensive laser copies of a
model's main book.*

◀ *The quality of laser prints, if
processed correctly, has improved
so much that it now rivals that
of expensive prints, and in some
instances is even better.*

Carter Smith

Height: 5'9"
Size: 6
Shoe: 8
Bust: 34C
Waist: 24½
Hips: 35
Hair: Brown
Eyes: Brown

ARiA
Chicago
Phone 312-243-9400
Fax 312-243-9020

BRIDGET
ETZKORN

quasi per

MUSTERSPIELE
Leicht wie ein Hauch
sind die übereinander
getragenen ärmello-
sen Kleider. Streifen
und Karos harmonie-
ren in zartem Creme-
weiß (Mod. 1G und 1B,
Anleitung S. 62). Die
Optik wird bestimmt
von langen Schulter-
bändern, die sich nach
Lust und Laune bin-
den lassen. Voller.
GéWé; Kropp; Drews.
SEIDENLEICHT
Ganz im Trend liegt
das gecrashte und plis-
sierte Seidenkleid
(Mod. 1H, Anleitung auf
S. 62) in kräftigem
Kornblumenblau. Hier
bestimmen die lan-
gen breiten Schulter-
bänder das Styling.
Den plissierten Seiden-
stoff gibt's zu bestel-
len über Anita Pletsch

speciale Bagni

18 Carino

CARTER SMITH

COMPOSITE ASSEMBLY

Your composite is another key component in your advertising campaign. Your comp-card is your business card. It communicates who you are, your body's statistics, a sampling of your capabilities in front of the camera, and your agency's logo with the name, address and phone number. How this information is arranged is decided by you and your agent, and the design possibilities are infinite. Modeling is a very creative industry, so make sure your card looks slick and professional, reflecting well on you and your agency.

Your best photos should be selected for your comp-card. This might mean you end up with only three photos on your card, but don't worry. If they sell you in an honest way, the card will do its job. Even with these "introductory" cards, the presentation has to be beautiful and professional, regardless of the quantity and color of the photos. Every model has to start somewhere. If you're new, the industry does not expect you to have an expensive, color, tri-fold comp. You have to develop at your own pace.

At the beginning of your fashion modeling career, your card will most likely be a standard 8 x 5$\frac{1}{2}$ inches in black and white, or a quick color laser card. Black and white is always less expensive than any kind of color card. Give yourself time to learn your trade and develop your ability to move and project your personality on camera before investing in colour; you will be much better six months into your career. Please do not use color photos on your hard comp until you are certain they will be current for at least a year and you have the time and money to invest in color. It can't be said too often: good photos are good photos, regardless of their color.

The kind of photos you use depends upon you and your market. What do you have to sell? How can you compete? Are you in a catalogue or editorial market? (Chapter 5 deals with these considerations in more detail.) Remember, common sense is crucial in putting together a good comp-card. Keep your advertising campaign in your mind constantly. Your composite is an extension of you and the agency — be sure that it sells you both.

◀ *A good comp-card is a vital part of a model's advertising campaign. Always use your best photos and don't invest in color until you have acquired some "timeless" shots.*

MATT KING

VERSACE
COUTURE

PARIS CANNES GENEVE ZÜRICH BASEL LUGANO LAUSANNE
BERN ST.MORITZ BRUXELLES ANTWERPEN KORTRIJK MOSC

Tim Gille

& DEREK

ARiA
Model & Talent Management Ltd.
1017 West Washington, Suite 2A
Chicago Illinois 60607

Height: 6'1½" Suit Size: 40L Chest: 41 Waist: 32 Collar: 16 Shoes: 11 Inseam: 34½ Hair: Dk Blonde Eyes: Gr

AGENCY PROMOTIONAL BOOK

Despite its name, this is another part of your advertising campaign. Every agency has a promotional piece of some kind. The bigger agencies produce "books," which are rather like collections of comp-cards. All the models the agency represents are featured in the book, and their photos are accompanied by their statistics and union standings. Some agencies are now using CD-ROMs too.

As with all the other parts of a model's advertising campaign, the cost of being featured in the book is borne by the model. However, the benefits to be gained from inclusion are priceless. Clients, agencies, and photographers at home and around the world "shop" for models from these books, so it is possible to get overseas bookings with minimal effort. The books also continue to promote you in your absence from a particular market, and are much harder to mislay than loose comp-cards.

Models are responsible for making their book submissions promptly. It is a serious matter to be late, as hold-ups can jeopardize the production of the book for everyone. Try not to be guilty of this.

HEADSHEET

Most agencies produce a poster with small head shots of each of the models it represents. This headsheet is sent out to photographers and all potential clients as a quick source of reference.

▲ *After photo shoots, it is normal practice for the models to sign a "release form," which gives the photographer/ client formal permission to use the photographs in specified markets. In the United States, the release forms are often written into the model voucher. Never sign any form without first speaking to your agent about what markets you should agree to – you might lose out on fees.*

WHERE DO PHOTOGRAPHS COME FROM?

If you're a new model and have no photos, how do you go about getting them?

In the United States the normal method of acquiring photos is through "testing." Originally, this meant that a photographer would have an idea for a shoot and ask a model to collaborate with him on it at his expense. Now, however, a model is just as likely to initiate the idea and hire a photographer (plus make-up artist and stylist) to shoot at her expense. In my opinion, this is good news: the model is not hanging around waiting for a photographer to do her a "favor"; she is in more active control of the test and her financial involvement usally focuses the attention of all concerned, resulting in better photos.

Your agent will advise you how to go about setting up a test and who to approach. In your role as "client" you can pick and choose who to work with, so make sure you view various photographers' books and find someone in whom you have confidence.

Testing is a great opportunity to extend yourself and take a few risks, especially if you are in a catalogue market with no editorial: you don't have the pressures and restrictions of a booking. Develop at your own pace and never compare yourself with anyone else.

If you are to get maximum value from your tests, preparation is necessary. Dancing and acting classes can help you develop the ability to move and emote, but simply practicing these things in front of a mirror is also beneficial. Photographers frequently complain that models "jerk" from one position to another on set. To train yourself out of this, stand in front of a full-length mirror wearing a swimsuit or leotard, and move slowly from one position to another, like a dancer. For head shots move close into the mirror and rehearse various emotions.

In any photo session it is essential to understand what is required. You must "become" the photo and direct every ounce of your energy toward the camera. No matter what your mood, you must always give your best and leave any unhappy feelings outside the studio. If you are not "into" a photo, it will probably "read" on to the film – even if the rest of the team has done a first-rate job. *You* are the key to the success of a photo.

A testing is just as important as a booking. Plan ahead, arrive on time, and have everything you need to ensure success.

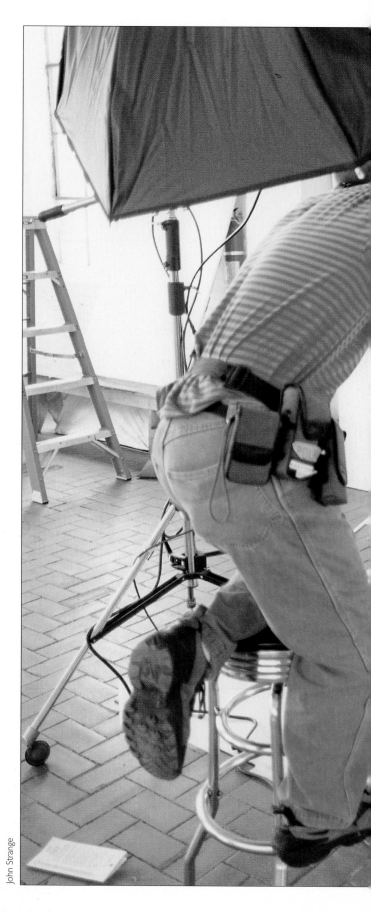

➤ *A team of new talent (make-up artist, clothing stylist, aspiring photographer and model) may pool their abilities to set up a shoot, and each will use the photos in their portfolios. Inset, far right: the finished photo.*

John Strange

Matthew Lipton

DIARIES

Your daily diary (date book) is also called your "industry bible," and it is vital to have a good one. Many agencies produce their own and include lots of useful information and addresses relevant to the modeling world. If you prefer to put together your own "bible," a Filofax is ideal as it has masses of pockets and can expand to fit your needs. The most important thing is that you have enough room to write on each page. (This demonstrates the power of positive thinking: you'll need lots of room to write down all the things you'll be doing!)

My datebook acts as a "center" for my life. Not only does it include the names, numbers and addresses of all my clients and agencies, but it is also full of reminders. It is a place to keep all bookings, appointments, business cards, and anything else I may need for reference. If I lost my datebook, I would be truly lost!

BRIDGET ETZKORN Model

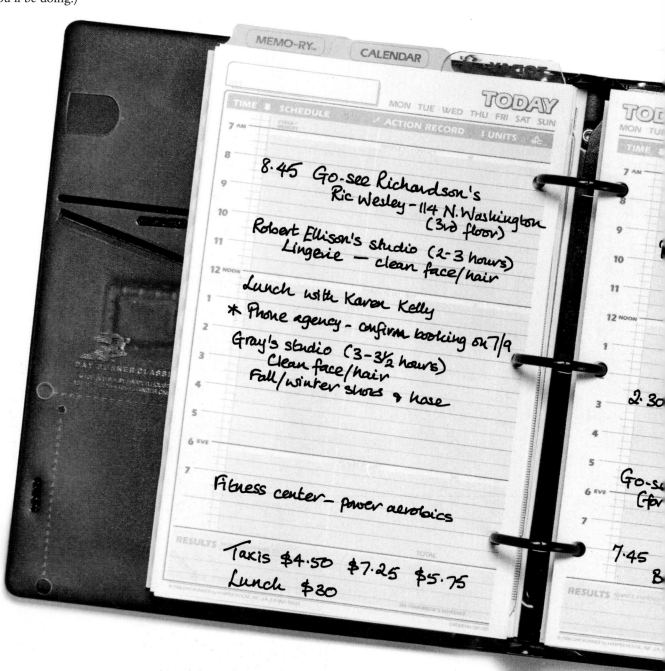

These diaries generally measure 6 x 7 inches and have a page a day. You should write every daily detail inside – in ink if definite, in pencil if provisional; this is all part of becoming organized and professional and the benefits are unlimited. For a start, it will remind you of your bookings and perhaps a note of how the client wants you to look – elegant, good nails, swimsuit, or whatever. It will also provide a valuable record for such things as audits: you can always look back in your diary to check queries about receipts, payments, and hours worked. If your agent is organizing an audition, always check the booking date to make sure that you don't have a conflicting engagement. At your bookings you should write down the name of everyone you meet – that way you'll always have a record of your interactions and build up a network of contacts. If your accounts department has any questions about a past booking, just look it up in your date book. Keep your daily diary close by and commit nothing to memory – write everything down.

One tip I have for models is to write down the names and positions of each person they meet at a shoot. The clients will be impressed that they remember their names when they return.

ALLAN BOYD Model

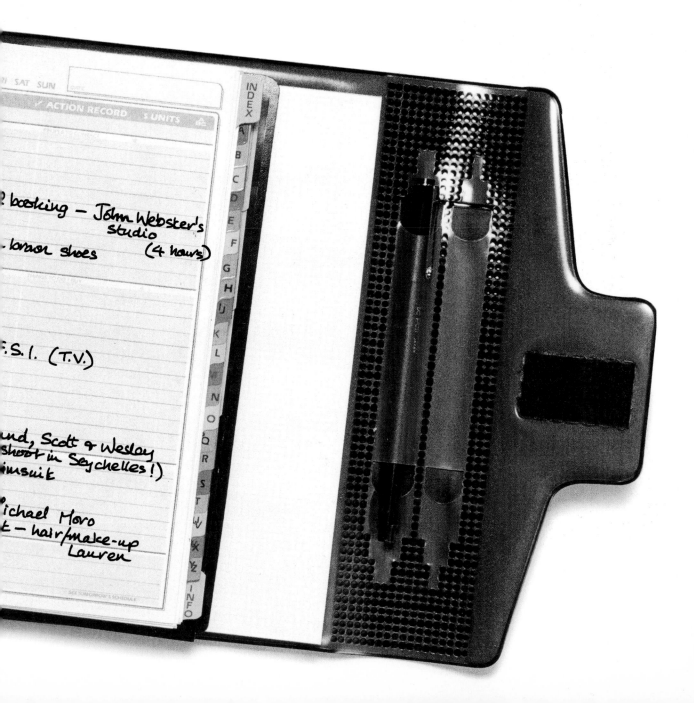

WARDROBE AND MODELS' BAGS

Ask your agent what is appropriate for the market with each client. Each market has its own requirements and some clients need to see the "look" they want in person. In places like Dallas and St. Louis they prefer models to dress up a bit with noticeable make-up. However, in places like London or New York, models tend to dress down with natural make-up.

Use your common sense. Everyone has his or her own style. Don't imitate others if it's not you. If you're not comfortable with your clothes, it will be difficult to sell yourself at go-sees or castings.

Models' bags carry the necessary tools for any normal fashion shoot. The needs will vary from market to market: there are even some markets (editorial) that don't require anything! Catalogue markets may require you to bring lots of things. With time and experience you'll learn what to carry and be able to anticipate what clients will like. For now, the basic requirements are:

WOMEN: DAILY BAG

- BRAS (seamless & underwire) and PANTIES (various styles; beige, white, and black)
- BODY STOCKING and TUBE TOP (flesh color)
- FLATTERING ONE-PIECE SWIMSUIT
- SLIPS (beige, white, and black) and DRESS SHIELDS
- PANTYHOSE (sandalfoot; flesh-colored, white, off-white, black) and SPORT SOCKS (white)
- LIGHTWEIGHT ROBE
- SHOES (heels and flats: white, bone, brown, black; clean white sneakers)
- ACCESSORIES (scarves, belts, jewelry)
- HYGIENE NECESSITIES (tampons, pantyliners, deodorant, nail kit) and SEWING KIT
- HAIR AND MAKE-UP BAGS (see Chapter 3)
- PORTFOLIO AND COMP-CARDS
- DIARY AND AGENCY VOUCHERS

Yes, this is a long, heavy list, but you won't be expected to have everything at the beginning of your career; however, you will be expected to acquire them gradually. Once established, you won't have to take everything listed above.

◀ *Model's bag for women – a selection of the items you should always carry.*

Michael Roberts

Men: Daily Bag

- **Underwear** (clean, white briefs)
- **Socks** (various colors)
- **Shoes** (clean, white, generic sneakers, black and brown dress shoes and casual shoes, cowboy boots and sandals)
- **Pants** (various colors and fabrics, including denim)
- **Turtlenecks and sweaters** (various colors and styles)
- **Shirts** (Dress, sports, and casual shirts; various colors and styles)
- **Swimwear** (boxer-style shorts and plain-color briefs)
- **Make-up** (base and powder to match skin tone)
- **Hair products** (spray, gel, brush, comb, etc.)
- **Sewing kit**
- **Hygiene necessities** (deodorant, razor, toothbrush and paste, contact lens solutions, etc.)
- **Portfolio and comp-cards**
- **Diary and agency vouchers**

In addition to bringing a good model's bag, a model should bring along with them a good personality. It can be the difference between being rebooked or replaced.

Mary Boncher   Agent

For many bookings, the client will provide the model with all of the merchandise. However, some clients may request that you bring one or several specific items. The professional model will bring these items clean, pressed and in good condition.

David Love   Agent

◀ *Model's bag for men – male models need to carry fewer items than women, especially in the cosmetics line.*

Beauty

Good skin care is important because your face is the canvas on which the make-up artist paints. Make-up should enhance your natural beauty, not overpower it. Less is more!

As a modeling agent dealing constantly with a variety of models, I know how vital a good beauty care regime is in self-presentation. That is why I invited three experts in these fields to collaborate with me in writing this chapter: Maureen Burke on skin care and make-up, Gary Novit and Clancey Callaway on hair. I have worked extensively with them and know they have experience in the salon and in the international photo and film industries. Their expertise is crucial to ensure that you get the most current and informed advice.

This chapter also touches on manicures, pedicures, dental work, personal hygiene, and plastic surgery – important topics in a professional modeling career. However, I stress that these subjects are only touched on here, as this is not a beauty book. If you want to read more, there are many other books that cover these topics in detail.

SKIN CARE BY MAUREEN BURKE

You can't place enough importance on good skin care. Your skin is one of the few things you'll have with you forever. Even though it may look flawless now, you must establish a basic skin care routine for preventive maintenance. It's never too early to begin, but do remember that what works for one person won't necessarily work for another as there are several different skin types.

If you are uncertain what skin type you have, you should consult a professional facialist. He or she will discuss skin types, skin care programs and product options. You may be able to buy similar products to those which are recommended, but at a lower cost from drug stores. For example, you may be able to use a special cleanser from the facialist in conjunction with a less expensive toner and moisturizer. Ask for recommendations if you're on a budget, and explain that you would like to spend the money you save on products by getting a monthly facial instead. In fact, a facial should be part of your skin care routine at least once a month. A good facial will clean the pores and smooth the skin without irritating it. Trial and error with your skin may end up costing you more in the long run, both financially and facially. For best results listen to the professional.

Remember, the skin is the canvas on which the make-up artist paints. It's your responsibility as a professional model to maintain it.

OILY/BLEMISHED SKIN
This is the most difficult skin to control. So many times oily skin is overdried and ends up dry, flaky and pimply.

If you spend a little more time taking care of your skin, you'll take a lot less time covering up its flaws. Better skin care, less make-up!

MAUREEN BURKE Make-up Artist

When it's moisturized to compensate for the dryness, more break-outs occur. It's a vicious circle, and the only way out is to balance the skin. Again, guidance from a professional is advised.

DRY SKIN
The main problem with dry skin is its tendency to flake. A light exfoliator is needed to remove dry skin, and it should be followed by an alcohol-free toner. You must then find the right moisturizer, usually one with a rich, creamy texture.

When traveling, the skin tends to dry out even more, so drink more water than usual and carry a remoisturizing mist which can be sprayed over or under make-up. A light peel once a month from your facialist will remove a layer of dead skin, creating a smooth surface.

If the lips are overdry, apply a vitamin E stick at regular intervals throughout the day. You may even use a soft toothbrush to lightly exfoliate the lips, but make

Norman Jean Roy

▲ *The skin must be thoroughly cleansed before applying a mask or make-up.*

Norman Jean Roy

▲ *For the best skin care results, cleanse in the morning and before going to bed.*

sure you reapply the lip conditioner afterwards. This will create a very smooth, full mouth – great for beauty shots.

SENSITIVE SKIN

When skin reacts badly to various things, it is described as sensitive. It may break out in hives, blotches or blemishes, and each person will have a different culprit. When trying a new product for the face, be it skin care products or cosmetics, always do a patch test on the inside of the arm by the elbow. If itching or redness occurs, you are probably allergic to it. Better a red patch on your arm than all over your face. You need to

pinpoint exactly what ingredients bother you. Fragrance and oils are usually the two biggest irritants, so steer away from products containing these ingredients.

COMBINATION SKIN

With combination skin, balance is all important. On occasion you may find that you will need to pay more attention to the "T" zone – usually the oiliest area – with a stronger toner than you would use on the rest of your face. Alternatively, you could use an oil-free cream in the "T" zone, using a richer moisturizer elsewhere. The presence of oil doesn't mean moisture is not needed.

Norman Jean Roy

▲ *Apply toner after cleansing to clean and tighten pores.*

▼ *Moisturizer should always be applied a few minutes prior to make-up application to allow time for it to penetrate the skin.*

Norman Jean Roy

GOOD SKIN CARE HABITS

Drink water constantly — at least 4 pints per day.

Eat a balanced diet.

Clean your face in the morning and evening using a basic skin care routine.

Use eye cream around the eyes to prevent fine lines. (Ordinary moisturizer may cause puffiness.)

Keep your hands off your face. Even if hands are washed, dirt and oils accumulate on the fingers and can contaminate the skin.

Always wear a sunscreen in addition to your cosmetics. Some cosmetics may contain sunscreen, but this gives only minimal protection.

Stay out of the sun.

Use a sponge to apply foundation for a cleaner, smoother, lighter finish.

Have monthly facials.

Do not squeeze blemishes under the skin — let them come out naturally or see your facialist.

You can never be too careful when it comes to skin protection.

MAUREEN BURKE
Make-up Artist

Johnathon Glynn Smith

▲ *Men's fashions in facial hair do fluctuate, but in general, it is always best to arrive at a booking or casting clean shaven. If another look is required, your agent should inform you of this prior to the date.*

MEN'S FACIAL HAIR

Men should arrive at a booking or casting clean shaven, unless instructed otherwise. There are two shaving techniques for men: the 'quick fix' electric shave or the traditional wet shave.

ELECTRIC SHAVING

1 Wash the face with soap or cleanser.
2 Rinse with warm water.
3 Pat the skin completely dry with a towel.
4 A pre-shave product may be applied to assist a close shave.
5 Use the electric shaver as directed.
6 A hot, damp towel may be applied to open the pores and reduce the risk of ingrown hairs.
7 Follow with aftershave or a cold-water splash to close the pores immediately.
8 Moisturize.

WET SHAVING

1 Wash your face with facial soap or cleanser, gently massaging the face with your fingers and warm water to create a lather.

2 Rinse thoroughly with warm water.

3 Apply shaving foam or soap with a brush to soften the beard.

4 With a double-edged razor, shave in the direction the facial hair grows. For a closer shave or hard-to-reach areas, stroke the razor in the opposite direction of the hair growth. (Rinse the razor between strokes for best results.)

5 Rinse the face with warm water.

6 A hot, damp towel may be applied over the face to open the pores and reduce the risk of ingrown hairs.

7 Apply aftershave or cold water to close the pores and prevent blemishes.

8 Moisturize the skin with a recommended moisturizer for your skin type.

▷ *Cleanse the face before shaving.*

Norman Jean Roy

Norman Jean Roy

It's a good idea to carry an electric shaver in your model's bag in case a "touch-up" shave is needed for a late booking.

MAUREEN BURKE
Make-up Artist

◁ *Shaving foam can be applied with the fingers or a brush.*

▲ *Follow the growth of the beard when shaving.*

WOMEN'S FACIAL AND BODY HAIR

Less is more in this case. There are several ways to handle each area of the face and body when it comes to excess hair removal.

BROWS

Tweezing is the best option in this area, as it is more efficient and accurate than waxing. Electrolysis is thought to be more permanent, but everyone's hair grows back differently. What works for one may not work for another.

BIKINI LINE, ARMS, UNDERARMS AND LEGS

Waxing is the best option for treating these areas. It is longer lasting and less irritating than shaving. Be sure to follow waxings with post-waxing gel to prevent ingrown hairs. Take care if waxing yourself; for best results seek out a professional.

UPPER LIP

Waxing is again the best form of hair removal, provided the wax is at the proper temperature; if it is too hot, blistering may occur. (Waxing any area of the body should be done well in advance of a shoot so that the skin has time to return to normal if slightly irritated.) Bleaching is not recommended for models, as it does not disguise hair in close-up shots.

SUN CARE

The best advice is to avoid direct contact with the sun at all costs. Sunscreen (ideally 30SPF) is a must for all areas exposed to the sun year round. Exposure to the sun can speed up the ageing process of the skin, causing wrinkling and age spots. You will also see immediate damage by burning. If exposed at midday, try to wear a hat (but don't ruin your hairstyle on a booking). When wearing sunglasses while working, place a tissue under the nose guard so as not to dent your make-up.

For a "quick fix," tanning beds are handy to create a healthy glow before a swimwear or lingerie shoot: they also assist in evening out tan lines. Remember, however, to use them in moderation. Alternatively, use a self-tanning cream that works naturally and evenly, but bear in mind that the results may be slower.

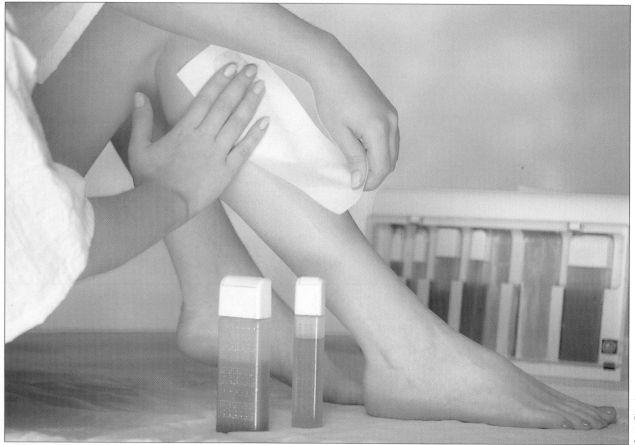

▲ *Waxing can be done at home using wax strips, but it's usually easier to have it done in a salon.*

Scott Chambers

Norman Jean Roy

▲ *Take care to protect yourself from the sun's harsh rays by wearing a sunscreen.*

MAKE-UP BY MAUREEN BURKE

Make-up should enhance your features, not overpower them, therefore less is more. When you go to a casting, the client wants to see what you really look like. Let your portfolio project your range of looks and show how diverse you can be. The following routine will help you to look your best at all times and safeguard your skin.

DAILY MAKE-UP APPLICATION ROUTINE

▼ START WITH CLEAN SKIN

Apply a light cleanser followed by an alcohol-free toner. Next, moisturize your face and put on a little eye cream. Finally, condition your lips with a vitamin E stick.

Norman Jean Roy

EYEBROW–SHAPING
Eyebrows frame the face and show expression. A clean brow line also helps to open and lift the eye.

▲ *Tweezing is preferable to waxing because you can control precisely which hairs are removed. If uncertain of how to shape your brows, don't just dive in – ask a professional's advice.*

▲ *While it's usual to remove only hairs under the brow line, a slight trim across the top may also be in order.*

▲ *It is a good idea to apply eyedrops before beginning make-up application.*

Norman Jean Roy

▲ CONCEALER

Apply concealer the same shade as your skin or one shade lighter to the inner and outer corners under the eyes, as well as to blemishes and broken capillaries.

▲ FOUNDATION

Test foundation color on your neck: if it disappears, it is the correct color. You don't want to see a color difference between the face and the neck because this creates a mask effect. Apply the foundation over the concealer and blend with a sponge, taking particular care around the jawline. There is no need to cover the neck if the color match is perfect. For a completely even appearance, apply a little foundation over the eyelids, lips, and ears.

Norman Jean Roy

▲ POWDER AND GUARD

Using a dome brush and loose powder, dust lightly over the entire face. Then take a sponge and apply a generous amount of powder under the eye area to act as a guard against shadow spillage.

▲ EYELINER PENCIL

Apply soft eye-lining pencil close to the lash line along the top lashes only. Then blend the pencil with a small brush to create a soft lining effect.

▲ MATCHING SHADE

Apply a matching shadow over the pencilled eyeliner to hold it in place.

▲ EYE SHADOW 1

Apply a light-color shadow over the whole eye area, from liner to brow.

▲ EYE SHADOW 2

Apply a medium color all over the eyelid, up to the crease, using a smaller brush to create a soft, smoky effect.

▲ EYE SHADOW 3

Apply a little of the medium shade under the lower lashes with a small brush to give definition. Always tap the brush before applying to remove excess shadow.

Norman Jean Roy

▲ BROW COLOR

Using a small brush, apply a faint amount of matching shadow to fill in any sparseness of the brows. Blend the color through in an upward motion with a brow brush.

▲ FINISHING THE EYES

Now that the eye make-up is complete, remove the powder under the eyes by brushing away the excess with a medium-sized brush. This will leave the eye area lighter, brighter, and cleaner.

Norman Jean Roy

▲ CHEEKS

On and above the cheek bone is the proper area for blush. A powder blush is usually easier to manage, and should be applied in a subtle shade in order to accent the cheekbones and add a little life to the cheeks.

▲ LIPS

Outline the lips with a natural-colored pencil to define the shape without drawing it. Fill in the lips using the same pencil, then apply matching lipstick with a lip brush.

For long-lasting color, blot with a tissue and dust lightly with loose powder to set. Reapply lipstick, using the excess left on the lip brush. Apply gloss only when needed for a specific look.

Norman Jean Roy

▲ EYELASHES

Curl the lashes before applying mascara. Apply mascara with the tip of the wand, going back and forth across the lashes for fuller coverage. Then brush the wand under and on top of the lashes for more coverage and separation. Using only the excess mascara on the wand, paint the lower lashes individually. Separate the lashes with a metal lash comb for the most natural look.

Norman Jean Roy

◀ THE FINISHED LOOK

Blot the entire face with a puff lightly coated with loose powder.

ETHNIC MODELS

The same make-up rules apply to everyone, regardless of ethnic origin. However, the colors used will vary according to skin tone.

People with darker skin tones often have problems in finding matching foundations: they are usually too red or too ashy. Asian skin tones tend to need more amber (yellow) tones, while Mediterranean skins usually need more true beiges.

For best results it's advisable to use a custom-blended foundation. (Although more expensive, it's worth the money to get it right.) For lighter skin tones, follow the step-by-step instructions given earlier. For medium skin tones, use medium shades wherever light shades are mentioned, and medium to dark wherever medium shades are mentioned. Gradually deepen the shades used as the skin darkens.

▲ *Apply powder with a large soft brush to create a diffused, even look.*

▲ *Blend eyeliner and powder eye shadow together well.*

▲ *Use a flat brush to apply lip liner following the contours of your lips.*

▶ *The finished look. The features are enhanced, yet look natural and fresh.*

Norman Jean Roy

NATURAL LOOKS FOR VARIOUS SKIN TONES

You want to see the effect of make-up rather than the make-up itself. That is why it's so important to find the perfect colors that work with your skin tone. If your make-up looks good in natural light, it will look good in any light, especially to the camera.

The color schemes shown below can be used in any combination as long as you use the correct shades for your skin tone. The most commonly used colors are warm browns, pinks, and peaches, but color schemes can be varied to suit your mood or to match your clothes.

Norman Jean Roy

▲ *Deep pinks and browns, shown here on African-American skin.*

Norman Jean Roy

▲ *Browns and beiges, shown here on Asian skin.*

Norman Jean Roy

▶ *Peaches and pinks, shown here on light skin.*

More dramatic make-up may sometimes be called for, depending on the look required for a shoot. The clothing, hair, make-up and photographic style should all work together to create a perfect photo for your portfolio.

Norman Jean Roy

Make-up can be glamorous and dramatic without losing its natural edge.

MAUREEN BURKE
Make-up Artist

Norman Jean Roy

◀ ▲ ▲ *A variety of natural but glamorous looks for various skin tones.*

BEAUTY EQUIPMENT

As a professional model, you should aim to have a condensed set of colors that will create a neutral look. If you have an allergy to certain brands of foundation, take your own with you to a shoot. It's also useful to include a few extras, such as a classic red lipstick, for more editorial shoots.

MODEL'S PROFESSIONAL MAKE-UP KIT

- TWEEZERS
- ASSORTED BRUSHES
- SKIN CARE ITEMS (cleanser, toner, moisturizer, cotton balls)
- EYE DROPS
- SPONGES
- POWDER PUFFS
- EYELASH CURLER
- CONCEALER
- FOUNDATION
- LOOSE POWDER (translucent)
- PRESSED POWDER (for touch-ups)
- 2 BLUSHERS (cool and warm matte colors)
- 2 EYE PENCILS
- 4 ASSORTED EYE SHADOWS (light, medium and dark matte colors)
- 2 LIP LINERS (cool and warm colors)
- 2 LIPSTICKS (cool and warm colors)
- MASCARA (usually black)
- NEUTRAL NAIL POLISH
- NAIL FILE
- RAZOR
- TOOTHBRUSH AND TOOTHPASTE

Michael Roberts

MEN'S GROOMING KIT

- CLEANSER
- EYE CREAM
- TONER
- MOISTURIZER – FACE AND BODY
- LIP CONDITIONER
- 100 PERCENT COTTON PADS
- ELECTRIC RAZOR AND TWIN-BLADE RAZOR
- SHAVING CREAM OR SOAP
- SHAVING BRUSH (FOR USE WITH SOAP ONLY)
- CONCEALER
- BRONZING POWDER AND BRUSH
- LOOSE POWDER AND BRUSH
- HAIRBRUSH AND GEL
- SCISSORS
- NAIL CLIPPERS AND FILE
- TWEEZERS
- TOOTHBRUSH AND TOOTHPASTE

*A complete male model's bag is
critical. A "must have" is pressed
powder in the correct shade for
your skin, as the wrong shade
can look terrible on film. Take time to
select the perfect shade for you.
If you want to be regarded as a true
professional, it's also essential
that you know how to
apply it.
Peeling lips are not an attractive
sight, so remember to apply lip
balm at night – that way you'll
always be ready for
close-up shots.*

LILIAN LAUREANO
Make-up Artist/Hairstylist

HAIR BY GARY NOVIT AND CLANCEY CALLAWAY OF VIDAL SASSOON SALONS

Your hair is an integral part of your career. In fact, it is usually the first thing people notice about you. If handled properly, it can be your claim to fame. The right cut and color can make all the difference in a model's career. For instance, there have been cases when going from long to short has taken an unknown model and transformed her into a household name. However, it isn't always that easy. As a model, the decisions you make concerning your hair are important business decisions. Just as a professional athlete needs the right coach, so a model needs the right stylist. The most important thing you must do is to find a hairstylist and technician you can trust and talk to – preferably one who understands the modeling business.

SELECTING THE RIGHT STYLIST AND SALON

Ask other models and your agency for referrals. They can give recommendations from personal experience. Shop around a bit – don't settle with the first salon you find. Visit several and request a free consultation. This doesn't have to be lengthy – just go in and get a feel for the salon and the stylist. Then, once you have determined the best salon and stylist, make an appointment long enough to discuss your needs before any services are performed.

HOW TO RECOGNIZE A TOP SALON

- Is it clean and well maintained?

- Are the staff courteous? Are they willing to answer all your questions?

- Are the staff wearing the latest hair and fashion looks?

- Is there a separate technical department?

- Do you feel comfortable in the salon?

- Is it part of a salon group which has salons in other cities? (This will allow your stylist to recommend someone else if you are away for long periods of time.)

For your first appointment, take along photographs of haircuts, styles, and colors you like. Make sure you arrive for the appointment with clean hair that is down and air-dried so that the stylist and technician can see its true personality. Sit down with the stylist and technician to discuss all your options and to prevent any

misunderstandings. In order to get maximum results, it is essential that your stylist and technician work together as a team. The cut directly affects the color or perm and vice versa. Once you have determined what your look is going to be, be sure to discuss it with your agent first. She will know if your chosen look is suitable for your potential clients. Once you are all in agreement, you can sit back and enjoy the experience of your new look taking shape.

SELECTING A HAIRCUT AND COLOR

Today, when it comes to cut and color, almost anything goes as long as it looks good. When it comes to selecting a style that's going to best suit you and your career, there are some basic things you should know about your hair type, facial structure, body proportions, and hair color.

HAIR TYPE

Your hair is either fine, medium, thick, coarse, wavy, curly, or a combination. While there are no hard and fast rules, the most important thing to keep in mind is to select a style that works with and enhances your natural texture. Trying to force your hair into a shape it's not suited for will only cause problems and make it much harder to handle.

If you want to alter the texture (by perming or straightening), you must discuss it with your technician first. The effects of perms (from a slight wave to tight ringlets) and relaxers (from soft curls to dead straight) can vary greatly. Note that these processes involve long-term commitment, so be sure you know exactly what is being done and that you really want it.

TIP

Don't be afraid to consider a perm or relaxer to help support the shape of your hairstyle. Under the right circumstances they can be great for a model.

▶*A distinct look, such as the one shown here, can make or break your career. Be sure to consult a professional hairdresser and your agent before making any major cut or color changes.*

FACIAL STRUCTURE

Your face is either oval, square, round, pear-shaped, triangular, oblong, or a combination. A good stylist can show you how and why a cut will or won't work with your face shape. He or she should also be able to show you how to adapt almost any cut to work with and enhance your facial features.

BODY PROPORTIONS

Your body is either short, medium, tall, thin, full-figured, or average. A haircut can look great for your face, but wrong for your body size. For instance, a super-short hair cut may look peculiar on a very tall model, while very long hair may overpower a smaller model. Your body size, shape and height are important factors in choosing a hairstyle.

▼ *The short fringe on this crop cut helps to create a more oval-looking face shape.*

▶ *The length of this bob cut flatters both the model's facial shape and body proportions. It's also perfect for her hair type.*

Norman Jean Roy

ETHNIC HAIR

While hair texture may differ among ethnic groups, the same two key rules apply: first, select a stylist and technician who specialize in ethnic hair, and second, select a style which works with your natural texture. Asian and Hispanic hair tends to be very coarse and straight, and looks best when kept natural and in prime condition. African-American hair ranges from very fine to coarse and from wavy to frizzy. At one time, most African-American models straightened their hair. Now, thanks to chemical advances, the possibilities are endless: hair can be relaxed, completely straightened, or permed.

◀ *A natural curly look is an attractive styling option when hair with this texture has been gently relaxed.*

▼ *Easy natural styling and versatility are the result of a great cut suited to this model's hair texture.*

For all types of ethnic hair it is essential to use good hair care and styling products. Those which work best on Caucasian hair may have no effect. Again, your stylist and technician should be able to recommend the right products for your needs.

TIP

No matter what hair type you have, once you have found the products that work best for you, keep them in your model's bag and don't hesitate to show them to the stylist at a shoot. It will make his or her job easier and help you keep the look you like.

Norman Jean Roy

Norman Jean Roy

MEN'S HAIR

The cut, color, and condition of a male model's hair is just as important, if not more so, as a female model's, simply because there tend to be fewer styling options for men. Thus, the same guidelines and rules apply, especially the need to keep hair freshly cut – usually every four weeks.

As you can see here, everyone has his or her own individual style. The key is to bring out your best while creating a look that is easy to achieve. A professional hairstylist will help you select a look that enhances your hair type, facial features, and body proportions.

Norman Jean Roy

▲ *Curly, long, short – even bald! Just as with
female models, there is no set look for male models. These pictures
show a variety of looks that are suitable for a range of jobs. The
critical thing is to look your best, and your hair plays an important
part. Your agent will help you determine the types of job that
are most appropriate for you.*

Norman Jean Roy

◀ Highlighting is one of the oldest and most popular coloring techniques. Here, three colors are being woven through the hair for a very natural effect. Many people prefer highlights because they enhance hair texture and require the least amount of maintenance.

▶ The highlighting technique known as "flying colors" was designed specially for short hair, so it is particularly good for men. Color is concentrated on the ends and can be as subtle or as strong as you want.

HAIR COLOR

Your hair color is as important as the cut, and most models' hair can use some sort of enhancement, even if only a subtle one. The key to success is always to have your hair colored professionally.

The color of your skin and the natural color of your hair will determine the range of color that your technician will recommend. It is important to understand exactly what you will be having done, the maintenance it requires (how often and how much), and how it will affect your hair and style. Below is a summary of the most common hair color products.

COLOR ENHANCERS

These enhance your natural color by making it richer, deeper, or brighter. Although the color can be subtle or dramatic, it contains no peroxide. The effects last 4–6 weeks, gradually fading as you shampoo.

COSMETIC COLORS

Ideal for covering the first signs of gray, blending with your natural hair color and adding shine and luster. These are semi-permanent colors containing a low volume of peroxide and last 6–8 weeks.

PERMANENT TINT

For those who want complete coverage of gray or even a dramatic color change. These colors add shine and body. They last 3–8 weeks, depending upon the level of color change desired.

BLEACH AND TONER

Especially effective on mature clients, who want to replace gray hair with a very soft blond look. Young clients who want to make a strong fashion statement also like this look. These products work best on short to medium length hair. Maintenance is approximately every four weeks. Regular haircuts and deep conditioning are strongly recommended for bleached hair.

HIGHLIGHTS AND LOWLIGHTS

Using pieces of foil, the technician weaves different shades of color into alternating sections of your hair. The final outcome is a natural (or dramatic) contrasting look: your individuality determines the result. Maintenance is approximately every three months.

HAIR CARE AND MAINTENANCE

Healthy, shiny hair doesn't just happen overnight: it requires a bit of maintenance. Be sure to trim hair every 6–8 weeks. Regular deep conditioning treatments at the salon and a proper home hair care regime will keep your hair in optimum condition. Your stylist and technician will be happy to suggest a daily and weekly regime that will work best for you. Below is a general list of hair care products and treatments.

HAIR AND SCALP TREATMENTS

Once-a-month deep conditioning (and scalp treatment if needed) can make all the difference in how your hair handles the stress of modeling. It's best if your salon has custom treatments that can be formulated to meet your specific – and often changing – needs.

MINERAL REMOVER TREATMENTS

Mineral deposits in water can affect the color, condition, shine, and malleability of the hair and also affect the scalp. Frequent swimming poses a whole other set of problems. However, all these issues can be resolved with the help of your hair technician. He or she can easily remove these unwanted minerals from the hair with one or two salon treatments.

GENTLE SHAMPOO

A mild shampoo that cleans the hair without stripping it of natural oils or drying the scalp.

PROTECTIVE SHINE CONDITIONER

A light conditioner which coats and protects the hair from damage. Good for fine hair too.

MOISTURIZING PROTEIN CONDITIONER

Helps moisturize hair that is dry or very dry. It contains ingredients to help restore moisture loss. Good for hair that has been chemically treated.

DEEP-MOISTURIZING CONDITIONER TREATMENT

A deep-conditioning treatment which can be used at home to supplement salon treatments.

▶ *Creative technical development, along with advanced products, means that permanent waving, relaxing, and coloring are no longer limited to one look. As long as the services are performed by a professional, the desired results should be achieved. Here, natural highlights brighten the model's hair and skin tone while softening her facial features.*

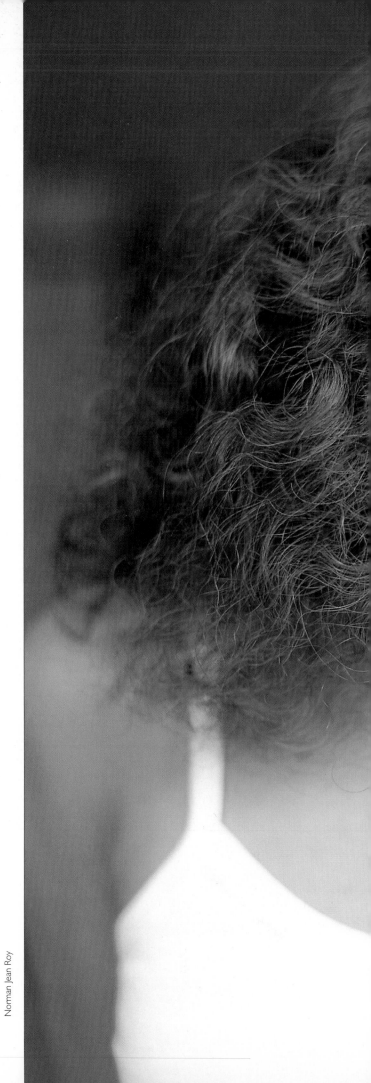

Norman Jean Roy

STYLING

As a model, your hair will be brushed, teased, spiked, crimped, curled, pinned, braided, or even made to stand on end if that's what the job calls for. With that in mind, it is best to keep your hairstyling regime as simple (and gentle) as possible when you are not working. Just as professional athletes need to rest their muscles, it's best to do as little as possible to your hair when you don't have to. One of the advantages of a good haircut is that it requires only minimal styling and will still look great.

BLOW-DRYING

Scrunching or tousling wavy or curly hair while either air-drying or diffusing it results in a very natural look. Blow-drying with a vent brush softens the natural texture for a more finished look. Straight hair usually looks better blown-dry with a Denman-style brush. While setting hair may be fine for work and special occasions, it really isn't advisable to do it on a regular basis.

STYLING AIDS

From mousses to gels to style fixes and hairsprays, there is a wide variety of styling aids that can subtly enhance or completely change your look. The key is to find the right products and to use them sparingly. Start with a little at a time – you can always add more as you work with the style. Here is a brief list and description of today's most popular styling aids.

HEAT-STYLING LOTION

A light spray product that is applied to the hair before blow-drying to prevent heat damage. It also helps to control flyaway hair and adds extra body and shine to the hair.

STYLING GEL

A liquid styling aid in a pump or tube which helps control and manage the hair. Great for slicking back.

STYLING MOUSSE

A foam product that adds texture and volume.

SHINE PRODUCT

Available in a variety of formulas. It is applied to dry hair to help add luster and shine.

FINISHING SPRAY

Aerosol or non-aerosol hairspray that is used to set the style.

Once you have your new hair look, you will begin shooting for your composite and portfolio. Meet with your agent to discuss the shots you need and the appropriate hair looks. Your agent may recommend photographers who will offer the services of a hairstylist for the shoot for an extra fee. Bear in mind that this is an investment in your career and is worth the extra expense. Make sure the photographer and hairstylist understand the looks you are trying to achieve. Your portfolio should show a range of hairstyles with your hair always looking healthy and shiny. Always be mindful of how your hair looks when selecting your photos. It is a good idea to periodically make new head shots, especially if you have changed your hair.

Marie Anderson Boyd

◀ *As a model, your hair will be subjected to intense heat styling from blow-dryers, hot rollers, and curling tongs. It will also be combed, brushed, back-combed, and coiffed in every conceivable way. When not working, it appreciates a rest from all this attention.*

CHANGING YOUR HAIR

Sooner or later you may be faced with the decision to change your hair. You may be at a casting where the client asks if you are willing to cut, color or perm your hair (whenever possible, it's best to go to castings with your hair as close to its "natural" state as possible – it gives the client a much better idea of what they are dealing with). Depending on the significance of the job and where you are in your career, it may be something you want to consider. However, you must discuss such a change with your agent before giving your consent. Remember, you don't have to make your mind up on the spot. If you and your agent are not sure, it's better to wait a day before deciding. Agreeing to a change and then reneging isn't very professional. Since there is a chance your regular stylist and technician won't be making the change, you should discuss it with them as well to be sure this new look will work for you and what has already been done to your hair.

QUICK TIPS FOR GREAT HAIR

Work with your agent, stylist, and technician to create your best look.

Be sure to have your hair trimmed every 6–8 weeks and maintain your color.

Have a salon deep-conditioning treatment at least once a month.

Supplement salon treatments with a good at-home regime.

Never cut or color your hair yourself.

Treat your hair gently.

Don't be afraid to try new things.

In general, mousses are better for fine hair and gels are better for thick hair.

▶ *For best results, naturally curly hair should be air-dried or gently blow-dried with a diffuser. To help control frizz and keep curls looking fresh, apply styling mousse or gel to towel-dried hair. Gently scrunch hair into place and diffuse or air-dry.*

▶ *For best results, blow-dry the hair in sections, starting from underneath. Use a brush to "wrap" the hair around the head.*

▶▶ *Used correctly, styling products are great for enhancing natural texture. Here, a dab of styling gel is combed through the hair for added control and hold without having to blow-dry.*

Norman Jean Roy

THE BODY BEAUTIFUL BY MARIE ANDERSON BOYD

MANICURE AND PEDICURE

I am indebted to Debbie Ciampi of Viva Nails in Chicago for giving me the benefit of her experience in writing this section. As this is not a beauty book, I have not given you a photo-by-photo explanation of a manicure and pedicure, but I will give you a few tips.

By this time in your life you should have a basic knowledge of how to care for your nails. If not, find yourself a good manicurist and learn. This is another investment to enhance your modeling career.

I recommend electric manicures, because their effects seem to last longer. Old polish is removed in the conventional way, then an emery board is used to file the nails into a slightly square shape (to strengthen the sides). Cuticle cream is applied around the cuticles, then a small, hand-held electric machine with a specially shaped tip gently pushes back the cuticles. The cream is removed with a paper towel, then cuticle oil is applied, again using the pusher as the massager. Next, nail cream is applied and a rotating electric brush scrubs the surface of the nails to clean them and remove unwanted residue. You then wash your hands, using a soapy nail brush to scrub off the creams and oil, and dry with a paper towel. Hang nails are clipped, then it's time for the polish: one clear base coat and two color coats. After ten minutes' drying time a clear sealer is applied.

A pedicure is basically the same process, but time is allowed for removing hard skin and massaging the feet.

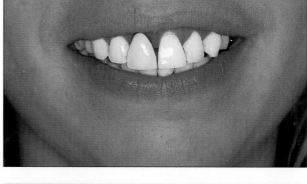

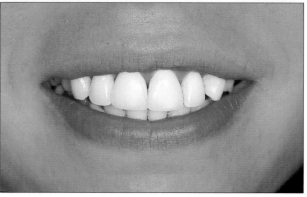

▲ *Gappy and uneven teeth are a common problem, but can be easily corrected. In this case, two front crowns have been replaced and tooth-colored plastic used to cover unsightly areas and give an even appearance.*

DENTAL CARE

This is by far the most common cosmetic work in the modeling business. Under harsh lighting and in close-up work gaps, chips, stains, discolored fillings, poorly fitting crowns, and badly placed teeth become more obvious. Some problems, like chipped or pointed ("fang") teeth can be smoothed down or rounded off very inexpensively. Modern dental materials now enable you to have white fillings, and the same substance can be used to fill gaps between your teeth. Porcelain laminate or plastic facings (bonding) can be used to cover ugly front teeth without doing any damage to them, but they can never be considered as permanent and may need replacing over the years.

Discuss exactly what you want with your dentist. Get at least two opinions and choose the most conservative approach first.

ROD MCNEIL Dental Surgeon

NAIL CARE TIPS

Keep polish on nails, even if it is clear – it keeps them strong and looking nicer.

Change polish weekly.

Keep hands well creamed, especially during winter months.

Put cuticle oil on dry cuticles at least once a day – twice during winter.

Don't remove any artificial (sculptured) nails by yourself – get a manicurist.

Never use any metal instruments on your nails – they scrape away proteins.

Whatever you do, don't be persuaded to have expensive and destructive crown and bridge work unless there is nothing else that can be done. Remember, teeth can make or break a model's career, so do not have any photos taken until your teeth do you justice. Ask your agent's advice and consult at least two dentists to get independent opinions and quotations – they may well differ in their advice.

Don't be talked into having expensive and irreversible crown and bridge work when there are so many other simple procedures.

ROD MCNEIL
Dental Surgeon

PERSONAL HYGIENE

It might seem silly to write about personal hygiene, but if it were unnecessary, I wouldn't mention it.

In many countries women with hairy legs and armpits are thought beautiful; this does not hold true in fashion photography. A female model should always shave legs and armpits before any photo session. As a safeguard, keep soap and a razor in your bag. Men should always be freshly shaved, unless the client has made a specific request for stubble – some clients like the one-day-growth look. Men should also keep in mind that they should be prepared to shave if necessary.

When it comes to menstruation, women should use tampons or slim pads that attach to the inside of panties. The old-fashioned pad and belt can show through clothing and spoil otherwise beautiful photographs.

Deodorants are always necessary for both men and women, although some clients in certain countries do not like perfumed armpits. Be sure to use a deodorant that will not spoil the client's garments. Women can wear dress shields for added protection.

Underwear may seem an obvious thing to wear, but you'd be surprised how many people don't. If you don't wear it, you must always carry a selection of underwear in your bag. It is not the stylist's responsibility to provide your personal undergarments.

Brushing the teeth! Yes, boys and girls, there are some people who do not enjoy this ritual. They choose to walk around with bad breath and bits of food stuck in their teeth – very distasteful and embarrassing. After eating, always check your mouth. And if you're going to do a tight shot with another model, please use a breath freshener: it can be very difficult for another model to concentrate with bad breath filling the air.

PLASTIC SURGERY

Do not have plastic surgery performed just because of your career. If you feel insecure about yourself physically and surgery will help, only then should you consider it. What if you have surgery just to please someone else and it goes wrong? What will happen to your career and yourself?

I have interviewed many models who have been advised by agents to have nose jobs, breast implants, chin implants, cheek implants... My goodness, there's a lot of free advice out there on how aspiring models can change themselves. I think that we should work with the original product and exhaust all other possibilities before you go under the knife.

If you have seriously considered the consequences and you choose to have cosmetic surgery, you must do extensive research and ask your agent or doctor to find you a reputable surgeon. The most common types of surgery are breast implants and nose alterations.

Models make more money if they do lingerie work, so the incentive for having breast surgery is often financial. The rate of pay is slightly more than usual, depending upon the item being shot. (Lingerie normally requires a 34B bra, often a 34C. The requirement is smaller for young teen models.)

Nose alterations are probably the most commonplace surgery. I know one model who had her nose done three times. The second time was because the first surgeon had not done a good job. The third time was due to the scar tissue not healing properly; the nose photographed strangely. We tried to talk her out of it on that occasion because we thought her nose had been through enough. She didn't listen, she went ahead. Fortunately, the final surgery was perfect – her nose looks great and you can barely tell there was any surgery. However, I know of some models who didn't have her success . . .

I do not encourage any type of surgery until you have really thought it out and are certain you wish to change something for yourself and not for your career. The dangers are too real to ignore, so please be very careful before you do anything to alter your appearance.

Be very careful in selecting your surgeon. You have to be able to talk to him. Get more than one opinion. Speak with the patients of your chosen surgeon. Ask to see before and after pictures of his surgery.

DR RICHARD CALEEL
President of the American Board
of Cosmetic Surgery

CHAPTER **FOUR**

Etiquette

How you conduct yourself in both business and social contexts is very important if you want to make the right impression and have people regard you professionally.

The following information on etiquette may seem obvious but, unfortunately, is often neglected. Please read it very carefully. You are establishing your reputation, so begin your new career with good habits. Common sense and consideration towards others are necessary elements for success, regardless of your career. As you enter and leave agencies, studios and client interviews, use the telephone or socialize, it is imperative that you keep the following points in mind.

IN THE AGENCY

The modeling agency is the nerve center of the business – a pressure cooker of constant activity. Phones ring continuously with inquiries from aspiring models, established models, new clients, current clients, make-up artists, hairdressers, photographers, art directors, messengers, talent scouts, out-of-town modeling agencies, parents, and friends. People flow in and out of the office. Bookers and agents within the agency also need to talk to each other. Everyone needs attention. Then *you* call or walk into the agency wanting attention… Do not take it personally if your booker does not have time to spend with you immediately. Yes, you are important, but if you do not have urgent business, you'll have to wait in line. However, we are not mind-readers. If you do have an emergency, then you must speak up, even if only to the receptionist; she'll know what to do or who you should speak to if your booker is swamped with priorities.

Bookers wear many hats, often acting as psychiatrists, surrogate parents, best friends, financial advisers, rental agents, best and worst critics, and chauffeurs, to name just a few. Imagine trying to be everything to everyone at once. It can be very draining. A simple "please" and "thank you" will work wonders with them. Be considerate and patient. The more considerate you are of them, the more they will be of you. Do not assume they will always solve all your problems. They also have their own to deal with.

Go in and out of the agency as quickly as possible. It is very disturbing to have a lot of people just hanging around. You should not have extra time on your hands. What else could you be doing? Preparing for a photo session? Taking a client out to lunch? Looking for a part-time job? Taking dance lessons? Working out at the gym? Taking acting lessons? Keep busy! (Can you imagine how many I.B.M. computers would be sold if the salesmen just hung around the office – not very many!) A model is a salesperson – you must always be out selling yourself. You cannot rely on your agency for everything. Do not make any calls on the agency phone unless you are given permission. Agencies provide many services, most of which are free. However, there are some for which reimbursement is expected: messengers, overseas telephone calls, faxes, portfolios and composites, rent for the agency apartment, or any other special service that may incur a high cost to the agency.

The agency is not a bank! Do not expect advances or interest-free loans. I've been in this business for 16 years now and it is amazing to me and my colleagues that models assume we exist to finance them. This is not true. You are responsible for your own career whatever line of business you are in.

IN THE STUDIO

You must treat a photographer's studio as if it were his or her home – very often it is. Remember that you are welcomed inside with the understanding that you will respect the property and the environment.

- Always be professional. Never forget that you are there to work no matter how friendly the atmosphere.

- You may offer to bring coffee or croissants to the shoot. You may be told it is not necessary, but the thought will be remembered and appreciated.

- Be prepared. You should always arrive with your requested wardrobe intact, pressed, and clean. Always bring your model's bag. Don't rely on any other person, such as the stylist, make-up artist, or hairdresser to cover for you.

- Personal stereos do not allow you to hear if someone is calling you. If you want something to pass the time while waiting to go on set, take a book to read.

- Arrive promptly at the time specified. You may develop a close relationship with various studios and they might allow you to arrive early. Always telephone first to ask – don't assume.

- Introduce yourself to everyone when you arrive. Be friendly. Shyness often comes across as arrogance. Write down the names and occupations of everyone in the studio: photographer, photo assistant, make-up artist, hairdresser, art director, client, and other models.

- Always ask before you take or use anything that does not belong to you.

- Don't send the photo assistant to run errands for you. If there is an emergency, always ask the photographer before getting an employee to leave the studio.

For me, being professional is always being prepared and respecting the client and their product. I go into each studio as if I'm seeing a new client, whether I've been there before or not. I never get too relaxed. I always bring more than requested. As for the client, if you don't like the clothes, you shut your mouth. Remember that you're getting paid – you're there to do a job, not to socialize.

MICHAEL COLLIANDER Model

- When changing, take care not to get make-up on the clothes you are to model. Get them on and off as quickly as possible and hang them up immediately.

- Don't sit, eat or smoke while wearing the client's clothes. They are often the only samples and have taken a long time to press.

- If you like the garment you are modeling, you may ask the stylist about purchasing it – after the photo session. Do not assume you can take it and do not pressure the client to give it to you. This will really put you in bad standing.

- Watch your step while walking on and off the set. There are many cords, lights, and other equipment that you could stumble on. Be careful.

- Don't chat with the other models on set. This is very distracting for the photographer and will interrupt his concentration. You can't hear him or his directions while you are talking. Excessive talk or gossip is always rude.

- Don't ever chew gum in the studio. This is an ugly habit. (Need I mention not to chew tobacco?)

- If you make any sort of mess, be it from food, drink, make-up or hair supplies, clean it up.

- Only use the telephone if absolutely necessary and be sure to ask first. Make your call brief.

- Ask the stylist about wearing dress shields to prevent perspiration stains.

- Drugs are absolutely forbidden.

Simple respect, politeness, and consideration are essential in a professional model. They make the difference between a short or long-term career.

GO-SEES AND AUDITIONS

Go-sees (go and see the client) or auditions are basically just that: you go and see, interview and/or audition with

Go-sees are informal interviews with potential clients. Several models may be seen at the same session, so be prepared to wait and take a book or magazine to help pass the time.

Michael McCafery

I look for personality during an interview. Someone who's self-assured and expressive is less likely to be stiff in front of the camera. I also look at what they're wearing to see if they have a sense of style and know how to wear clothes.

DALE STACKLER Art Director

an established or potential client. These opportunities arise in various ways:

- The agency might call a studio to introduce you in a "general" go-see.

- A client may call the agency and inform them that they have some time available to catch up on who's new in town.

- A client may call the agency to request a go-see for a specific job he is casting (he is searching for a certain "type" of model).

- A client may call in response to your composite received in the mail from your agency.

- A client may have seen you at a social function and request a professional interview with you and your book.

THE CLIENT INTERVIEW

Interviews are tough in the beginning, but they'll get much easier with experience.

Arrive on time and dressed as the agency has requested. (You'll have a better chance of getting the job if you walk in looking like the photo they have in mind.) If the agent did not make a suggestion on how to dress, ask her. If she does not know, dress midddle of the road – not too high fashion and not too casual.

When you are greeted at the door, smile, say who you are and why you are there. (For example, "Hello, I am Annette Cusick, from Aria, Chicago. I'm here for the Armani casting.")

If you are asked to have a seat, sit down. Sometimes you may not have a place to sit; it is not uncommon at go-sees for there to be many other people waiting. Try to smile at everyone and say hello. (Don't be dismayed if no one responds. Most likely they are as shy or nervous as you are. Remember that shyness can come across as arrogance.) You might start up a quiet

conversation with someone. (Be careful here – loud conversation can distract someone trying to work. Also, no gossip!) Bringing a book or magazine is also acceptable. You should be prepared to wait anything from a few seconds to an hour and sometimes longer. There could be many reasons for the delay. Be patient. If you have another go-see or booking, tell the receptionist very politely. Possibly you'll be allowed in next. If this is the case, apologize to the other people waiting and say thank you. Believe me, it will inevitably happen to them too.

More than likely a client will have seen a lot of people before you and will probably see many after you. You may all have similar physical characteristics. What makes you different from the others? What do you have to offer that they don't? Why should the client book you? Know the answers to these questions before you go into any interview. You are there to sell yourself.

When your name is called, stand up and follow the person who addressed you into the interview room. Smile and say hello to the people who are doing the interviewing. Shake hands firmly if you choose to (a limp handshake is a turn-off). State your name and which agency has sent you. Wait for an invitation to sit down. (Some clients will do the interview as you stand. Don't worry – this is not unusual.) Be prepared to hand over your book for inspection.

An interview may last from thirty seconds to thirty minutes; you cannot predict how long or short it will be – just flow with it. Normally when you go into an interview, everyone is under pressure to find the right model(s) as quickly as possible, to book them, and to produce the rest of the photo session while juggling with the other daily activities. It is not unusual for a client to have a couple of auditions for different jobs on the same day.

If time allows, take the opportunity to bring out your personality – naturally! You don't have to go into a tap dance or sing – just be yourself. That way the client has a better insight to you and your photos. You know when you click immediately with some social contacts, but others take a little longer to warm to? This is all to do with personal chemistry. Photographers and clients are like that too. Sometimes you'll immediately get on and sometimes it will take longer to warm to them. Your mood and their mood are factors in determining the success of the interview. Regardless of their behavior, always remain friendly, calm, and professional. (Remember you are selling a product – yourself. If you believe in the product, they will too. Sometimes it won't happen immediately. Don't push too hard! This is also part of establishing your reputation.)

After your book has been seen and handed back to you, the interview is probably over, depending on the conversation. Leave behind your composite with the interviewers. If they do not want your composite, don't be hurt. If you're not appropriate for that job, your card will only confuse them when they're trying to decide whom they will book. Stand up, smile and say, "Thank you for your time. It was a pleasure meeting you." Shake hands if you're comfortable doing so and walk out of the room.

Photographers and clients often have incredible memories. They may not book you for that particular job, but they will keep you in mind for the future. It is not uncommon for weeks, even months, to go by before the photographer or client phones the agency and requests to see you again for a new job being cast. I cannot possibly tell you everything about how to interview on your go-sees or auditions in this chapter. Take the information that you've read and apply it to the situation as you feel appropriate. This book gives only guidelines, not mandatory rules.

ON THE TELEPHONE

Communication is another crucial key to success. When you are calling a place of business, do not make it a guessing game as to who you are and why you are calling. Every second you waste is time – and time is money. You'll make quick friends with people if you are direct and don't waste their time. Say immediately who you are and why you are calling. I received a phone call one particularly hectic day and the caller said, "Ummm, ughhh, hello. Ummm, ugh, I was walking down the ummm street yesterday with my friend, Sally, and ummm ughhh we were looking at the magazine covers and ummmm ughhh I mean Sally said she had an aunt who knew a girl who ummmm ughhh knew a photographer. . . ." I said, "Here, maybe I can help. Are you interested in becoming a model?" She said, "Ummm ughhh, yes! How did you know that?" I then explained to the caller how our agency handles new models.

Can you imagine going through several of those conversations a day while trying to take care of a highly pressurized business? I have made appointments with people immediately just because I liked the way they handled themselves on the phone. The telephone call is also part of your sale. If you cannot communicate before you get an interview, I wonder if you'll be able to communicate in the interview itself. If you are nervous, practice with your friends; it may feel silly, but you'll learn the habit of preparing yourself for all sorts of telephone conversations.

Try to get on and off the telephone as quickly as possible, but without babbling. Excessive conversation can be distracting to the flow of business at that moment. If you are making an inquiry, be ready to write down the information. Don't call people and interrupt their answers to your questions with, "Oh, can you hold on while I find something to write with?" They have many other priorities in their day, so try not to irritate them. Some examples of direct, business-like inquiries are given in Chapter 1. Of course, the more familiar you become with people, the longer the conversation. You needn't become a robot. Just develop good habits when dealing with people who have little time to spare and are under a lot of pressure.

Make a list of things to discuss so that you have an agenda once the conversation gets going. Always be direct. Don't waste the client's time or yours.

TOM BIEN Model

Michael McCafery

SOCIALIZING

Socializing is an integral part of the modeling business. It does help to be seen in the right places, but proceed with caution. If not handled properly, it could have a negative effect on your reputation. Now here's the tricky part – what is "proper?" Everyone marches to a different drummer and what is proper for you may not necessarily be proper for another person. Numerous business situations will present themselves: in restaurants, studios, hotel rooms, and so on. Who pays the bill? Should you drink alcohol or refuse drugs? What should you wear? Should you go off your diet to make a client more comfortable? Should you sleep with a client in order to get a job?

If you have issued the invitation – to lunch, dinner, or whatever – you should pay the bill. If you've been invited, your host should pay the bill. If it was a mutual decision, each person should pay his or her share. If there is any doubt or discomfort, just ask, "Shall we go Dutch?"

John Welzenbach

It is not considered unprofessional to have a glass of wine or a cocktail with dinner. Only you know how much alcohol you can handle and a professional would never drink too much while doing business. Listen to yourself.

Drugs are bad for your skin, your mind, your hair, your body, and your general health and well-being. They are destructive elements in a professional model's career. If they are offered to you, politely refuse.

What you should wear depends upon the situation. If you are dining at a smart restaurant or going to a formal event, dress up; for a more relaxed atmosphere, dress casually. Be comfortable with yourself and the way you look. Clean and simple is always the best choice. Tattered or dirty garments are entirely unprofessional. Avoid items that are too trendy and do not wear heavy make-up. Always remember that your clothing is an extension of yourself and is perceived that way by others. If there is any doubt in your mind, ask your agent what is appropriate.

Parties and social gatherings can present great temptations in the way of food and drink. Don't feel pressured by people offering you cheesecake when you are on a diet. They should understand, and even if they don't, it is not impolite to refuse their offers. Remember, it is possible to have a good time and still watch what you consume.

No matter how old, how experienced or how professional you are, there will always be tricky situations to handle. Whatever your behaviour, be aware of it and accept the consequences.

Don't ever have sex with someone who promises you a job in return. Chances are you won't be given the job and you'll simply get a bad name for yourself. Modeling has a promiscuous reputation (not entirely unfounded), but the best rule is always to follow your instinct. Behave professionally and others will respond in kind. Power has a strange way of affecting people. For many it means exerting power over others. I believe it is important to have power over yourself. Let other people worry about themselves. If you don't want to do something, don't do it. If you do want to do something, go ahead. Always keep in mind that your behavior is part of your reputation. How do you want people to remember you?

If you are out socializing and a client doesn't remember you, don't be hurt. There are hundreds of models and it's difficult to remember everyone. Defuse any embarrassment by reintroducing yourself. Don't be surprised if some people pretend not to know you; this happens a lot. I laugh when people do this to me – if it makes them feel more important, who am I to spoil their fun?

Insecurity can also alter people's behavior. Modeling tends to breed insecurity, possibly because the future is always uncertain. Regardless of your environment or what is going on, insecurity can pop up at any time. It's understandable that you may be overwhelmed by some people when you are just beginning your career. The more experienced you are, the more secure you should become.

Photographers, hairdressers, make-up artists, clothing stylists, and models are all hired for their abilities to fill the client's job requirements. Sometimes you will succeed, sometimes you won't. Try to keep a positive attitude and treat people as you want them to treat you. Yes, this is an old adage but you'll be amazed how well it works. It's very important to get out there and try. You'll eventually find a system that works for you.

COURTESIES

Acknowledgements of appreciation are not old-fashioned! Something as simple as a card, a rose, a cigar, or a basket of fruit just to say "thank you" to someone special is always appreciated and your thoughtfulness will be remembered. It doesn't have to cost a lot. The small investment you make will undoubtedly come back to you over and over again.

If you have made a *faux pas* or mistake you regret, a simple gesture of consideration can easily persuade someone to forgive your foolishness. Our model, Devin Devasquez, inadvertently double-booked herself to two major clients just as her career was taking off. It was a bad blunder and involved letting one of the clients down – in fact, that client vowed never to use her again.

In this instance, I suggested that Devin send the client some flowers by way of apology. They received no immediate acknowledgement from the client, but several weeks later that same client called me to offer Devin more work, saying that her thoughtful gesture had been appreciated.

If you find yourself in a spot like this, the least you should do is to write a brief letter of apology to the client (in some cases your agent might insist you write the letter in her presence so she can approve it). The form of your apology (letter, flowers or whatever you think appropriate) depends on how well you know the client. Don't be nervous of saying sorry for your mistakes – a graceful apology can work wonders.

Apart from being a good way to make useful contacts, socializing is also a great way to relax. But beware getting too relaxed – you don't want to end up saying or doing something you might regret later. Reputations are fragile things.

CHAPTER FIVE

Modeling Opportunities for Men and Women

PRINT OPPORTUNITIES

"LIVE" OPPORTUNITIES

I could have written a book on this subject alone – there is so much for you to know. The first thing to be aware of is that modeling can be broadly divided in two: print work and "live" work. Within these two areas there are many different opportunities.

James Caulfield

In this chapter I describe the most available opportunities around the world, and give you enough information to decide which area sounds appropriate and feasible for you. Keep in mind that the more involved you become in this industry, the more educated you'll become. As a result you'll be able to make better decisions and have more control over your career.

Back in the 1980s I could easily have broken down modeling into several well-defined categories. That is not the case today. Every day there are more and more people getting into the business. As a result, there is a constant influx of new talent around the world with new ideas and advertising strategies. They are constantly experimenting and changing the standards. Sometimes the new talent and their ideas are accepted, sometimes not. You must keep up with new developments in the industry in order to compete worldwide. You must also be versatile to give yourself maximum opportunities for

▲ ▶ *Advertisers frequently show their garments on attractive people in sophisticated situations – but not simply to show the clothes to advantage. They believe that potential customers like to imagine themselves in similar situations, so these advertisements both inspire and fulfil fantasies.*

My advice to models, regardless of their area of interest, is to realize who they are – what it is that is special and unique in them – and to capitalize on those attributes.

JOHN WELZENBACH Photographer

work. Remember, there are hundreds of markets to experiment in (each with its own terms and definitions). This chapter deals mainly with fashion modeling.

The term "fashion" refers to clothing and accessories. To work in this area you must be a sample size.

FEMALE – STRAIGHT
    5ft 8in – 5ft 11in
    Size 6–8: 34B–24–35
FEMALE – FULL-FIGURE
    5ft 8in – 5ft 10in
    Size 12–14: 38C–28–39

MALE
    5ft 11in – 6ft 1in
    Size 40R: 15½in neck; 32in waist;
    34in inseam

Modeling clothes is an art. You must learn how to walk, move, and show off the clothing to stimulate the sale. When potential customers look at a model, they are generally imagining themselves in that same outfit. Clothing is designed to appeal to those leading specific lifestyles, and to those who simply aspire to them. In this way clothing can both create and fulfil daydreams and status. The model's image must enhance the image of the clothes and this must be consistent throughout the campaign: the model, the mood, the clothing, the art direction, and the advertising placement. Keep in mind that if you do not get a job, your "look" may have been considered inappropriate for that particular shoot. Do not take it personally. Perhaps you will have the right image for the next audition. Fashion modeling encompasses everything from glossy fashion magazines (editorial) to mail-order catalogues, from live shows for *haute couture* houses to "rag trade" promotions.

PRINT OPPORTUNITIES
CATALOGUE
This is exactly what the name suggests – photos of specific merchandise, from sweaters to saucepans, presented in a strict style in a catalogue. It is crucial to

move gently and slowly in catalogue shots, always keeping the line of the garment in mind. (The garment has normally been pressed, pinned, taped, clamped, and sewn into place.) Not surprisingly, the models normally look so stiff that they resemble store window mannequins. Each photo is accompanied by "copy" – written information about each item on display.

Mail-order catalogues were originally aimed at the rural shopper unable to get into town to buy clothes. As home shoppers became more comfortable with the concept of catalogue shopping, their tastes became more sophisticated. As a result, the catalogue producers had not only to keep current with fashion, but also had to produce attractive, up-to-date catalogues. For years now city dwellers have also been using catalogues to do their shopping, so the market has opened up considerably, creating more jobs for the catalogue model.

Within the field of catalogue work, there is a growing need for models who are not of stock size or appearance: full-figure, ethnic, and older models. The modeling agency is constantly attempting to fill the needs of its clients. We scout and sign models according to their specifications. When we fill our quota for that type, we move on to the next area of need. If an agency tells you, "We already have a couple of your type," keep in mind that these are specialized areas. Agents are in business to make money. Sometimes we lack diplomacy, so please accept our apology in advance if we are too abrasive. We really do try to be delicate when we say no to a model. If you're sensible, you won't take it personally. Take it as a challenge. Timing is everything. Don't be easily discouraged. Whenever you are among the minority, you will inevitably meet competition for those few openings.

James Caulfield

FULL-FIGURE MODELING

This really began in America, but it's slowly creeping into other countries. Two years ago my agency in Chicago did not represent any full-figure models. We now have two and both are earning a very good living. They model exactly the same clothes as stock size models, but in full-figure sizes. I have been at many American conventions where European agents have teased me about scouting for full-figure women. Now some of those agents have begun looking for themselves!

Full-figure modeling tends to attract older women, but agents are particularly on the lookout for young women aged 19–30 who are 5ft 8in–5ft 10in and wear a size 12–14.

> *Being a full-figure model is not about being a large woman with a pretty face. Just like regular size models we need to have nice features and proportions. It is also important to eat a healthy diet and stay fit because full-figure does not mean flabby.*
>
> ASHLEY CARMAN   Full-figure Model

Fadil Berisha

> *Like many full-figure women, I wasn't always comfortable with my body. Once I accepted my size, I realized that big can also be beautiful. Now I'm very confident and proud of my figure.*
>
> ASHLEY CARMAN   Full-figure Model

Fadil Berisha

Norman Jean Roy

ETHNIC MODELING

"Ethnic" usually refers to people of African-American, Asian, Indian, or Hispanic origin. The demand for ethnic models is growing tremendously and new markets (not least South Africa) are offering many opportunities in this field. However, modeling is in a constant state of flux, so don't be disheartened if you don't fit the bill immeditaely – your turn will come.

Ethnic models tend to work in fashion, full-figure, part, older, and product print modeling. If you are one of the ethnic types listed above and are unsure about your suitability for particular markets, consult an agency.

Being considered a "non-traditional ethnic" has advantages as well as disadvantages. Some might feel you're too much of one thing or not enough of another.

PAUL K. Model

African-American models must avoid being type-cast. They have to push against the boundaries to get away from always being shown as sporty and exotic.

ELO Model

As a model of African, Chinese, Spanish, French, and Scottish ancestry, I can work in many different markets. But clients do have a problem categorizing me.

MATTHEW Model

Anthony Edwin

Being mulatto, you don't fit into the African-American or the white category. White clients try to use African-Americans who aren't too ethnic looking. They are usually interested in lighter-skinned and classical-type features. African-American clients usually opt for a definite ethnic look so that they appeal to their market. Mulatto models can fit into a variety of jobs, and may also be cast as Hispanics. You'll be rejected for jobs that require a specific ethnic type.

RITA CRAIG Model

◀▲ *Being an ethnic model does not confine you to working only for ethnic markets. If you are a real professional, you'll be able to get work in all areas of modeling.*

Interesting Development Photography

OLDER MODELS

This category is increasingly sought after because there are increasing numbers of elderly people in the world. These people have money to buy products and they want to see themselves represented in advertising. For example, a woman in her forties might not be persuaded by a 20-year-old promoting a hair-coloring product; similarly, it is very difficult for a man of 75 to see himself in a business suit modeled by a young man of 25. As a result, older people increasingly promote clothes and products that their generation is interested in.

Older is relative, isn't it? But generally speaking, people above their mid-twenties are "older" in the modeling industry. They are more likely to be "real people" photographic models (see page 110) rather than to work in fashion. The market need for older people is based upon the population. Product campaigns are designed to appeal to the population of particular communities, so very few teenagers would feature in advertising campaigns targeted at a predominantly retired audience.

I'm always looking for the perfect figure – someone who can adapt to all areas of catalogue – men as well as women. My idea of a professional is someone who moves well. I don't mean posing. It's the ability to change body movements naturally (especially as there are photographers who don't give good direction), being able to interpret and project the mood necessary. They have to be able to do their hair and make-up well. Also, it's crucial that they have a good disposition. Nobody wants to work with an unpleasant person, especially if you're on location for a while.

JIM KIRCHMAN Fashion Director

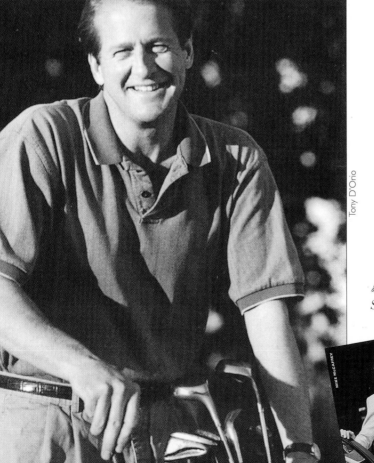

Tony D'Orio

▲ ◀ ▼ *Older models' comp-cards, showing Sharon Scully and Ed Hoban.*

EDITORIAL MODELING

The term "editorial" applies to a section in a fashion magazine *and* to a type of photography. Confusion can arise here because you can actually have a catalogue photographed in editorial style. Generally, editorial photography has a much freer style than that used in standard catalogues; it avoids the traditional, mannequin-like poses against a seamless backdrop. This looser style allows much more creative input.

Editorial photography in magazines is a more subtle sales approach than that found in standard catalogues. The editor of the magazine decides on the photographers, models, clothing, accessories, and locations. He or she is familiar with the basic concept, layout, picture quantity, and size before the photo session. However, during the photo session the talent involved will most likely influence the basic concept. As a result, there is more freedom of movement and expression by everyone.

The art director will often design a spread around finished photographs, utilizing them in a way that will lend the greatest appeal to the page layouts. The copy is less noticeable in editorial. Pick up a fashion magazine and turn to the editorial section. Look at the movement of the models in conjunction with the clothing. Look for the copy. See how small it is. You almost have to search for the designer, store, and prices of the garments. Now look at a Sears or Montgomery Ward catalogue. Look at how stiff the models and clothing are in comparison with the magazine. The copy is obvious. You immediately know what the fabric is, the colors the garment comes in, and how much it costs.

◀ *Static catalogue style shot in a studio.*

▶ *Studio catalogue shot in editorial style.*

Editorial is so much more believable. People like to fantasize themselves in more editorial-type situations – skipping, jumping, spinning, whatever – it's a natural movement. Standing straight up with your head cocked to the side and your mouth half open is unnatural. People identify so much more with natural movement.
Good editorial models must be able to move well and understand that, although we are shooting in an editorial style, we are first selling clothes. They have to create the mood and attitude necessary, and still be able to show the detail of the clothing. They have to be actors, creating a shot that will make people stop and look and relate. They must be able to put themselves in the shoes of the person that they are trying to reach.

ANN O'MALLEY Advertising Director

◀▶ *The photographs on these pages show how subtle changes in pace can present the same basic outfit to three different markets.*

> *Even when an ad is shot in editorial style, it's not truly editorial because it is still a controlled piece of work. In an ad you have certain constraints complying with what the client needs you to do.*
>
> DAVE FLEISHMAN Photographer

Norman Jean Roy

▲ *Editorial-style catalogue photo shot on location.*

Norman Jean Roy

Ken Zame

▲ ▶ *The difference between catalogue and editorial work is shown in these two shots. The model above is stiffly posed, whereas the model on the right looks far more natural, almost as if he's unaware of being photographed.*

A major difference between catalogue and editorial work is the time element. Catalogue sessions are normally produced to very tight deadlines; there are many garments to shoot in a short period of time. In editorial sessions there is generally a little more time allowed for the creative process.

The editorial sections in magazines provide models with prestigious exposure at minimal cost to the publishers. Fees for editorial work are comparatively low, especially for up-market magazines like *Vogue*. However, models (and agents) accept the low rates because the work is so prestigious and the tear sheets are a valuable addition to a model's portfolio — almost a guarantee of future work. Money is the main reason for doing catalogue work. With luck models may get a catalogue or a catalogue section which is photographed in editorial style and pays catalogue rates. This way you get prestige and money!

FASHION ADVERTISING

This is another sales approach, involving photographic advertisements which focus on the clothing. They are similar to catalogue work but they are single separate shots placed in appropriate magazines. Generally the designer's name is prominent with a list of places that sell his clothes. Advertising fashion shots can be photographed in catalogue style or editorial style. Each shoot demands different approaches. The art director and the client decide the image necessary and plan the project accordingly.

Fashion photography began in Europe, and Europe still sets the standard around the world. In the past you could easily pick out European fashion advertisements in American and Japanese publications. Now these markets are becoming more educated about fashion, and consumers are responding to the more European editorial approach. In fact, sometimes now when you look through magazines it can be hard to tell editorial spreads from a series of fashion ads.

In the U.S. and Canada, the rates for fashion ads are the same as for catalogue work. In the U.K., the fashion rate is much higher, but the shoot may last only one day. Catalogue work may last several days, so in the long term it is much more lucrative. The only time fashion modeling overtakes long-term

Bruce Weber

VERSACE
COUTURE

▲ *This is an example of fashion advertising, which is often rather subtle in its approach — the wording is discreet and additional product information may be non-existent or given in tiny print.*

catalogue assignments is when a model is contracted to work exclusively for one client, such as Chanel. The client has to pay an exclusivity fee on top of the daily rate to compensate the model and her agent for other work offers they will have to turn down.

If you land an exclusive deal, you've really hit the jackpot, especially if the client produces a variety of merchandise — clothes, perfume, jewelry and so on — because each product in the range is open to separate negotiation.

PRODUCT PRINT ("REAL PEOPLE")

Any person you see promoting a product in a photo, such as Dove soap or Marlboro cigarettes, is a character model. (Of course, fashion is a product, but it is an area of its own.) Think about all the other non-fashion products available and the variety of people used to promote them. The product may need someone who looks like a fashion model, or possibly a short, heavy-set man with a funny, expressive face, or maybe a woman in her forties. The sky is the limit!

I have often suggested to people that they try product print, usually because they do not have the right look for fashion modeling. It's amazing to watch their reactions: they behave as if I have suggested a vacation in the salt mines of Siberia. It is a great pity that so few people understand the importance of "real people" modeling – the exposure it can give and the kind of money that can be made.

Unlike fashion modeling, product print offers many other opportunities. You have to use your common sense in approaching it; look really closely at magazine ads and billboards, examine the product and the type of person advertising it. If you resemble that person in look and age, consider photographing yourself in that way.

Many models have two books: one fashion and one product print; both should be prepared with equal care. Be thorough and watch the details. If you are not a fashion model and you wish to pursue product print, the strategy is the same – just change the concept to match your target market.

Marc Hauser

Paul Elledge

Tough clothes for tough customers.

"Real people" is an area of modeling that is often unknown to aspiring models. I think it's sad that so many models are sacrificing a very lucrative career because they only want to be fashion models.

JOHN WELZENBACH
Photographer

OSH KOSH B'GOSH
UNION MADE IN THE U.S.A.

Marc Hauser

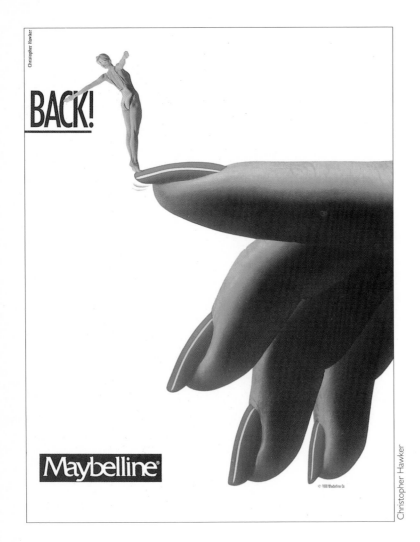

Christopher Hawker

BACK!

Maybelline

© 1990 Maybelline Co

Christopher Hawker

◄ *Absolute perfection is necessary to be a successful hand model, as close-up shots expose the hands to intense scrutiny.*

PART MODELING

Widely used in commercial product print, as well as fashion work, part modeling involves separate parts of the body: hands, feet, hair, eyes, teeth, breasts, lips, and so on. Some models make an extremely good living as part models. Some fashion models do it as an addition to their everyday bookings. Be warned though – part modeling is extremely difficult to stay in, mainly beause everything always has to be *perfect*.

How do you know if you've got what it takes to be a part model? A good sign is if people constantly remark on your hands, legs, or whatever. (It is also a great asset if your joints are supple as you may be required to hold awkward positions for a long time under hot lights. Believe me, part modeling is not as easy as it looks.

It is not unusual for hand models, whose career is literally at their fingertips, to have their hands heavily insured. This is not as silly as it may sound. For example, a cut finger from, say, chopping vegetables could easily result in loss of work and possibly lead to a scar that could permanently damage a career.

I have seen far too many composites with terrible part shots on them. One model had wrinkly hands, dry and flaky skin, and her nail polish was chipped. Another model had the focus on her hair, which was horribly dry and broken, and sprayed out so far that you could see through it. This amazes me. Do these people see advertisements photographed like this? Of course not. Please do not pursue this area if you are not "camera ready." This means that the body part has to compete against established models, be in perfect condition, and ready to be photographed. Check with your agent and ask to see composites of current part models – this should give you a good idea of the standard of perfection required.

Note that part models in the U.S.A. and Canada earn exactly the same rate as fashion models: having only part of the body photographed does not mean that part rates are paid. In the U.K. the rate is about two-thirds.

NUDE MODELING

Nude shots are most frequently requested in product advertising and editorial work. The agency will always inform you in advance and no pressure will be exerted on you to accept. If a photographer and/or client asks you to strip at a shoot without prior warning through your agent, don't do it! Such a request is completely unethical, so phone your agent immediately and get her to deal with the situation. Note that the fee for nude or topless modeling is frequently triple the normal rate.

A great model will project a feeling to the camera that will belie her true personality. For example, an ingénue will display sophistication, a wild girl will appear reserved and demure.

STAN MALINOWSKI Photographer

ILLUSTRATION MODELING

Illustration models pose for drawings or renderings wearing clothes, holding a product, or perhaps posing for a book cover. Before the days of photography, illustration was the only printed form of fashion advertising. This method is still used occasionally as it is much less expensive than photography. It also gives the illustrator and/or manufacturer the freedom to change the appearance of a garment, and even change the model's face or hairstyle, if they wish. The pay for illustration modeling is comparatively low, but it is still fashion work and can lead you into other areas of modeling.

Norman Jean Roy

▲ *Nude modeling can encompass anything from up-market calendar shots to down-market tabloid newspapers. Never strip for a shoot unless it's agreed in advance with your agent.*

MALE MODELING BY DAVID LOVE

While their supermodel sisters have become household names, male models have always lurked in their shadows, facing issues both similar and different from their female counterparts. The most noticeable difference is that the modeling industry is one of the few businesses that greatly favors women, both in terms of the quantity of work and the amount of money earned. Women can make quite a bit of money fairly quickly, while men have to invest more time in the business. Another oddity is that men work more as they get older, which is the complete opposite of the youth-obsessed women's market.

Most men get into modeling between the ages of 18 and 30 and claim to have started as a fluke. Many were "nagged" into modeling by friends; others were simply "discovered" by a talent scout while standing in line at the grocery store or hanging out at a coffee shop. No matter how a male model gets started, he has a long, hard, and exciting road ahead of him. You have to invest money to make money, and many men hold a flexible second job while their careers are developing. Some are lucky enough to have their careers take off right away, but the majority of male models lose money during their first year in the business.

The men's fall/winter shows start in Milan the beginning of January. This is an incredible opportunity for the model to be seen by photographers, magazine editors, and press from around the world. After Milan, the collections are seen in the other major fashion markets, including Paris, London, and New York. In July the models hit the runways for the spring/summer shows.

DAVID LOVE Agent

Whether a male model starts out in a small market like Grand Rapids or in a large market like New York City, he ultimately needs to spend time in Europe, where he can test and have a better chance of getting editorial tear sheets because there are more magazines and opportunities for men in markets such as Paris and Milan. These fashion capitals are also the homes of some of the world's top designers, who help dictate styles and trends and recruit aspiring male models to help in creating an image for their designs. Each year

My experience as a model taught me that having a great face is not the only key to the industry; having confidence, personality, and the ability to think for yourself is what opens the door.

SEBASTIAN
Aria Men's Director

hundreds of new male models flock to Europe for the autumn/winter collections in January and the spring/summer collections in July in hopes of being one of the chosen few with that special something which catches the discriminating eye of a top designer or photographer. Sometimes it takes only one photographer or designer to use a male model for a special project or editorial to launch his career and send him on an unforgettable journey which often includes travel to exotic locations and parties with movie stars and royalty.

As with all careers, there is a downside to the life of a male model. Relationships become almost impossible to sustain when you are living out of a suitcase and rarely in one place long enough to unpack. Some men get a lot of criticism from friends and family who don't understand the business and are quick to condemn them for pursuing a "woman's job" or to stereotype them as "brainless" or "gay."

When you come down to basics, modeling is a competitive business where a lot of money can be made and only the strong will survive. You must also remember that the product you are selling is yourself. This involves staying in shape, being professional, and exuding personality and emotion in front of the camera. If you can do all these things, you will increase your chances of having a successful career as a male model, but don't forget that there are many others who can do the job just as easily as you.

As far as my own personal experience is concerned, I was "discovered" by Marie Anderson Boyd while waiting tables in Chicago. I continued to wait tables while I put together my portfolio in anticipation of going to Milan. I studied all the international fashion magazines and practiced facial expressions and movement in front of a mirror every night. Once Marie felt that I was ready both emotionally and professionally, I got on a plane and headed to Milan for the fall/winter collections. That journey from Chicago to Milan was far more than a long flight: it was like going from playing catch with my dad to playing in the World Series.

Three days after arriving in Milan, I took a train to Florence for my first job, which was a fashion show for

Michael Voltattorni

storing my food outside on the window sill to keep it cold.

I continued to test to strengthen my book, and after three months of pounding the pavements in Milan, I was off to Tokyo on a two-month contract with an agency I had met while I was in Milan. My trip to Japan was financially successful, but physically and emotionally disastrous. I lost a lot of weight because I was too big to fit the clothes for the Japanese market. Meanwhile, my parents, who could never understand the modeling industry, were far from supportive, which made things difficult as I had always tried to please them. When my contract ended I returned home to screw my head back on and regain the weight I had lost.

After a summer of saving money and preparing myself physically and emotionally for the business again, I headed to Miami, then back to Milan, and finally to Paris. I spent a lot of time in Paris doing the shows, editorial work, catalogue, and TV commercials. Life was exciting, but at the same time I was tired of living out of a suitcase and not being in one place long enough to develop any real friendships, let alone relationships.

I decided to stop modeling, so I called Marie from Paris to let her know I was coming home to settle down. One thing led to another and I became the men's fashion director first at Aria and then at Look in San Francisco. This goes to show that the life of a model can lead to many exciting careers in the industry, from working as an agent or photographer to being an editor or an art director.

Maurizio Bonas. It was an incredible high...the lights, cameras, clothes and so forth. Little did the buyers, photographers and stylist know that when I got off the runway I was back in old jeans and sweater on the train to Milan where I continued to eke out an impoverished existence with my two room-mates. Trying to save money involved staying in a *pensione* that made the Y.M.C.A. look like the Ritz, washing my few clothes with shampoo and drying them on the radiator, and

If your dream is to be a model and you meet the physical requirements (see page 16), then go for it. Believe in yourself and be prepared to work harder than you have ever worked before. Good luck, and never forget where you came from or sacrifice your values.

"LIVE" OPPORTUNITIES

RUNWAY MODELING

Runway work involves modeling clothes in a live fashion show. It is a great way to begin a fashion modeling career as it does not require much money. However, it does require a lot of skill.

Runway models must move with the grace of a dancer, project the image required, and make people want to buy the clothes. In print you can rely on the lucky split-second photograph to capture a look for you; this is not the case on the runway. There is no room for cheating. This is a form of fashion that you must practice as a dancer practices his or her art. You should take all types of dance class and also practice at home with music in front of a full-length mirror. As they used to advise years ago, practice walking around with a book on your head. Practice changing quickly from tennis shoes and shorts into heels and a sophisticated suit. You may even want to practice with other models at home. *Everyone* needs practice. As designers expand their lines, you have to be able to carry off every type of clothing possible, which means changing clothes and mental attitudes very quickly. This will make you very competitive.

Unless you work in a small market, it is difficult to get into runway modeling because it requires so much technique, skill, and sense of timing. Added to this, runway models are very territorial and rarely welcome newcomers. However, once you have established yourself as good and dependable, you will be readily accepted.

> *Women's prêt-à-porter (ready-to-wear) shows occur twice a year: the fall collections are shown in Milan, London, Paris and New York, starting in Milan in March and ending up in New York in April. In October through the beginning of November the same thing happens with the spring shows. Twice a year in Paris (end of January and end of July) the top designers show* haute couture. *These clothes are one-of-a-kind and very expensive, made for a special clientele.*
>
> SUSANNE JOHNSON Runway Agent

Many photographic models become even more established through runway modeling. Becoming a designer's private model can earn you prestige as well as money. Models who move in a couture designer's circle are known as his or her "cabine." The designer teaches the models exactly how to behave, regardless of the environment, which ensures that the designer's public image is always consistent. The opportunity to work for an *haute couture* house comes about very infrequently, so once in, models guard their positions jealously. Note that runway models tend to be more slender than print fashion models, although the basic sizes are the same.

Runway auditions are quite different from print auditions. For a start you must be able to walk well,

Andrew Lamb © Vogue, The Condé Nast Publications Ltd.

and few print fashion models can. Clients
will expect you to appear dressed in their
style of clothing, with appropriate hair,
make-up, accessories, and attitude. You
must really do your homework before
you audition for runway modeling. Ask
lots of questions until you become
familiar with the work and style of
various designers. Personality and
character are major factors in any sort of
modeling, but they are particularly crucial
in runway work. That audition is your
opportunity to convince clients that you
understand their concept, that you will be
prepared, able to handle the responsibility
of their merchandise, and not buckle
under pressure. Any mistake you make
could lose money for a designer. You
must always be aware that a great deal of
money and many months of preparation
have been invested in a show. The
designer needs assurance that you are the
right person to make the sale.

Backstage at fashion shows is often a
scene of mass hysteria. Even if you are
doing a marvellous job, your client could
end up screaming at you just to release
some of the pressure. Remain calm,
confident, and understanding – that is
also part of your job. Once you've
worked for the client and established
trust on both sides, you could have
steady employment for years.

Wardrobe is crucial in modeling,
particularly in runway work where you
have a diverse clientele to appeal to. If
you don't have a decent wardrobe, you
may have to borrow a few things until
you do. The more work you do, the more clothing
you'll get, as designers frequently give away their garments
at the end of each season. One of the perks of being a
model is that you can also buy designer clothes at
wholesale prices.

Whether you are wearing the clothing or taking it to a
job, you should always be prepared and the garments

*Attitude is the
key to being a
good runway
model. You have
to "feel" the
garment.*

TANIA CROSS
Runway Director

should be fresh and clean. Even if the clients don't request
that you bring shoes, stockings, and accessories, you'll
score extra points if you do. They'll see how professional
you are and how much you appreciate the job.
Remember that any time you go to an audition or
interview you are a sales person. What kind of image do
you wish to project? Clothing is the wrapping on that
package. Make sure it reflects your intention.

◀▲ *Runway modeling requires more skill than first
appearances suggest. You must be able to walk well and
move fluidly along a narrow runway, showing the clothes
to advantage, but never looking down at your feet.
Fashion shows are finely tuned events – one slip could
ruin months of hard work.*

SHOWROOM MODELING

"Rag trade" manufacturers produce mass-market fashions which they promote within their own show-rooms. These shows are very informal and frequently employ very young and inexperienced models, but experience of the runway is very helpful; equally, show-room experience is great practice for the runway. Whether modeling lingerie, sportswear, fur coats, or formal attire, it's imperative that models know how to move.

Showroom models are superhuman! They can endure long hours in high heels on cement floors with a constant smile and a warm greeting.

KATHY NEDVED Agent

In small companies, models' duties may also include answering phones and making coffee. In large companies, models may only be expected to model the clothes. The agreement you come to with the manufacturer is individual; you may be employed full time or simply on a freelance basis as and when shows arise. Manufacturers like live shows as they create a much stronger impact for buyers and/or the press than mannequins, and they can get a real feeling for how the garments move on a human being.

These shows are strategically placed around the changing seasons. Buyers purchase fall and winter lines during the early summer, and spring and summer lines during the fall and winter months. Showroom models are generally busiest around holidays. The money is not especially high, but it is steady work and offers opportunities to build up a network of contacts. You can always add to your income by pursuing other avenues in modeling.

Norman Jean Roy

INFORMAL MODELING

An informal model, also called a "trunk show" model, is usually hired to promote a store opening or a new line of clothing for a designer. Such models might be seen in a boutique, shopping mall, at a lunch, or even in a private home. These models must be able to walk well and talk intelligently about the line they are promoting in case the client asks questions, such as, "Is that dress comfortable?"

Some informal models travel for a specific company, others are freelance. Those attached to a company could be involved in a production as big as a choreographed music show.

PROMOTION MODELING

Promotion models are usually freelance and sell products as well as clothing. They are hired a short time in advance by the fashion or public relations directors of department stores. Promotion models are the ones who ask if they can spray you with a "sensational new cologne" or press you to try on "Europe's latest design." The money is relatively low, but it can usefully supplement a new model's income. Promotion modeling is another opportunity that many people ignore, but like anything else in life, you can work it to your advantage.

FIT MODELING

A "fit" model is one whose body is exactly the right size for a designer's sample garments. A perfect fit is essential and the model's body size cannot fluctuate even a fraction, as measurements (from shoulder to elbow, from elbow to wrist, and so on) are so precise. Fit models might have to stand for hours and hours as the designer and assistants pin and sew garments to their bodies. Models could spend days watching them piece together a new line and then decide not to continue with the production.

This may not sound like very glamorous work, and perhaps it's not, but it can lead a model into other areas of the industry. He or she may be chosen to do the designer's ads or runway show – anything is possible. Although this type of modeling does not pay a lot and is extremely demanding, it is a valuable education: fit models learn a lot about fabrics, design, and construction of clothing, which helps them to understand how to work with the garments after their completion.

CONVENTION MODELING

This type of modeling is really the most difficult. Convention models are on their feet all day, often in huge, purpose-built convention facilities, selling products they might have seen for the first time only that morning to vast numbers of potential customers. Convention models generally earn more per day than editorial, fit, illustration, and promotion models but, unfortunately, this type of modeling is the least respected by many people in the fashion industry – they feel that conventions are beneath them.

Kathy Nedved is an agent who specializes in supplying models for trade shows and conventions, and she knows the business inside out.

"Trade show and convention models are not only attractive; they must also be very upbeat and positive when working so close to the public. Although many may think it is an easy job, the truth is just the opposite. Hosts and hostesses (the most common bookings) are simply attractive men and women who help to promote an individual company and/or products by passing out literature, speaking to the public, and assessing interested and potential buyers, but they may also act as secretary/receptionist, taking messages and confirming meetings. These individuals must be energetic and always willing to run an errand or handle a situation when called upon. Nowadays, most hosts and hostesses dress in 'corporate style' so that they look like an actual employee of the company. Occasionally, however, you may still seen an attractive model dressed in a mini-skirt or bathing suit, depending on what the company has requested.

"Convention models may also be employed as demonstrators and narrators. For these tasks they must be very knowledgeable about a particular product, which they demonstrate or narrate (describe) to crowds every half hour during the eight-hour day. These people are paid much higher rates than hosts and hostesses because they are required to memorize a script. Sometimes they use an 'ear' – a tiny hearing device connected to a tape machine – which allows them to hear the script and repeat it as it is heard. This is rather like speaking while being spoken to and takes time to become accustomed to. They also have to pray that the batteries don't fail in the middle of a presentation!

"Interpreters have an important part to play at conventions. They usually speak at least two languages and translate what is being said to their host. This is rather like being a tour guide, as you have to walk the visitor through each demonstration, explain technical situations, and answer questions.

"Each of the trade show roles described presents its own difficulties. Dealing with people is always harder than standing in front of a camera or walking along a runway. The public can sometimes be downright rude and it takes a strong person to shrug it off and keep smiling. I believe that trade show and convention models are the most well-rounded in our industry, and they certainly have the toughest skin. Although the job is not easy, it can be exciting to fly around the country, seeing new places and experiencing different things."

When convention models do a good job, they are happily rehired by clients, often many months in advance. Can you imagine having secure bookings several months in advance? Few fashion models can boast the same. So, if you're of strong character, enjoy public contact, and are a great salesperson, convention modeling could be for you.

When I'm interviewing a trade show/convention model, I'm considering her looks, personality, and height. She can't be too fashion pretty because she has to be approachable. She must be very outgoing with an upbeat personality, and 5ft 6in to 5ft 8in tall. A comp and résumé are important tools in a model's success. Convention rates in Chicago range from $175 to $1000 a day, depending on a model's abilities and skills. The rate is often higher if she can use an "ear" prompter.

SHIRLEY HAMILTON
Agent

CHAPTER **SIX**

Modeling Around the World

Travel Tips

Foreign Markets

Traveling to new markets will not only enhance your career, it will also increase your confidence and open your eyes to different cultures.

TRAVEL TIPS

Before we go any further with this chapter you must keep a few critical factors in mind. While updating the information that follows, I was amused to get conflicting reports from agents operating in the same market. This, however, is the nature of the business and you must do your research thoroughly before you travel anywhere.

One fact that all of us agents did agree upon is that the business is always changing. Years ago you could predict peaks and troughs in the various international markets. Nowadays it's more difficult. In the late 1980s,

BEFORE YOU GET ON THE PLANE

Telephone the agency at your destination and confirm details of your accommodation. Leave a note of the address and telephone number with family and/or friends in case of emergency. Ask the agency how much the taxi fare from the airport should be and whether you should tip the driver. Although taxis are more expensive than public transport, they are convenient and lessen the anxiety of finding your own way.

If a member of the agency is to meet you on arrival at the airport, make sure you have his or her home phone number, or that of the agency owner – just in case.

Don't overpack! Traveling light will get you in and out of planes and trains with minimum hassle. Also, if your luggage is stolen or lost (it can happen), you won't lose too much.

It's a good idea to wear (and take with you) lots of black clothes. Black can carry you from one occasion to another with a few accessory changes.

Remember to pack your hairdryer and travel iron, plus electrical adaptors and/or plugs.

Have at least $100 (including some change for telephones) in the currency of the country you are visiting.

Make sure you get a flight that arrives during daylight hours – it makes it easier (and less intimidating) to find your way into town.

When making your reservation, ask for a seat near the bulkhead (the partition dividing the cabin), or near emergency exits, as these areas usually have more leg-room.

Allow at least two hours' checking-in time when traveling overseas – it can take ages to get through all the formalities.

for example, South Beach/Miami was not an important venue; now, however, it's a major shoot location. Other places on the up in the mid-1990s include Phoenix, Arizona, and South Africa, which is becoming a major competitive market for models and clients.

In the modeling year, the seasons tend to blur into each other: with the worldwide exception of Christmas and New Year's Eve, and the European exception of August, business is business. Work opportunities arise all around the world, so if male or female models have a great book with great cards, they'll find work pretty much anywhere they want to go. Only supermodels like Christy Turlington do not need to be concerned with where the market is.

Chasing after work is generally the lot of new models and unmanaged models: in fact, it's for them that I wrote this chapter. It can offer valuable insights to each market or city but do remember that it's only a general guide and should not be used as the only source of information.

Imagine this situation: you arrive for the first time, alone and nervous, in Japan. You're a long way from home and you don't speak the language. You have to get from the airport to the center of town, but which way do you go? Where is the taxi rank? Is there a bus service? Every sign you see is written in Japanese. Help!

It can be very disorienting to arrive in a foreign country whose language and culture are quite alien to you. Is it all right to hail a taxi in the street? Should you tip the driver? Is it safe to go out alone after dark? Is English widely spoken? These are just a few of the

labels on map: iburg, Milan, Tokyo, Osaka, ohannesburg, Sidney, Melbourne

▲ *Travel to overseas markets is essential if you want to achieve real success as a model. This map shows the main fashion centers around the world.*

AT YOUR DESTINATION

In these days of high security, many countries have armed guards strolling through their airport terminals. If you've never come across this before, it can be quite intimidating. Don't be concerned – they're there for your protection.

Part of the fun of travelling to foreign parts is seeing how other people live and eating unusual food. But there are several precautions you should take to ensure you stay healthy and able to work efficiently, for example:

- Always drink bottled mineral water and use it for cleaning your teeth. Your whole system can be easily upset by foreign tap water.

- Avoid eating food from street merchants – it's not always hygienically prepared and stored.

ON THE PLANE

Air travel affects different people in different ways. Taking the following items in your hand-baggage may help to lessen any discomfort you might experience.

Chewing gum will help to "pop" your ears.

A large, plastic bottle of mineral water will help prevent dehydration.

An aerosol can of Evian water is very useful to spray on your face to prevent dry skin. Apply a light moisturizer and lip balm if you do experience tightness.

Wear minimal make-up; your pores have enough to cope with on the plane, so don't overburden them – your skin might break out.

Brushing your teeth will help to refresh you during long trips, so take toothpaste, toothbrush, and dental floss.

Eye drops will soothe dry, irritated eyes.

Remember to carry any medication or vitamins you're taking.

Keep your passport, visa, camera, and any precious jewelry with you. Ideally, try to avoid traveling with anything expensive.

Good reading material and/or a personal stereo help to pass the time.

At the risk of upsetting airlines, I have to say "Avoid airline food." It is high in salt and preservatives, which can cause water retention, slow digestion, and constipation. Order a vegetarian meal (when you buy your ticket) or take some fresh fruit and vegetables to eat, but ask the airline first – some don't allow you to take these things on board.

---

questions that will inevitably cross your mind – but once again I must stress that the best line of defense is to be prepared. Before you leave your home territory, contact the tourist office of the country you intend to visit and get maps and brochures. While nobody expects you to master every foreign language, you can learn a few essential words: please, thank you, where is..., the days of the week and numbers. The local people will appreciate your making the effort, but most of all, you will feel more confident if you don't have to rely on sign language alone.

I've tried to cover (briefly) everything you'll need to know to have a trouble-free journey, but there is no substitute for first-hand experience. Ask other well-traveled people for their advice; even if they're not models, they can still give lots of useful information.

JET-LAG

On long-haul travel (any journey involving a time difference of more than three hours), jet-lag can be a big problem. Unfortunately, there's no sure way of dealing with it. Until your body becomes familiar with the effects of jet-lag, it's difficult to know what to do about it. My best advice is to try and stay awake until the appropriate time to sleep at your destination. If you must have a nap on the plane, keep it brief.

FOREIGN MARKETS

The following section has been compiled to help you understand what markets are available to you. It is in no way intended to replace the advice and recommendations of your agent. Information changes all the time as the industry, markets, and agencies are constantly changing. Even though I made many phone calls to agencies all over the world and spoke with many experienced models, I found a wide variety of opinions on each topic.

This chapter gives a breakdown of twenty-four different cities, and the information under each is divided into the following categories:

MARKET

It is impossible to outline all the types of modeling you will encounter in each city. I have concentrated mainly on fashion modeling, but each market usually has a little bit of everything. It's up to you to be resourceful – find out what each market has to offer and prepare accordingly. Note that the seasons vary from market to market and may even be different for male and female models. Check these things out when you arrive.

PORTFOLIOS

Wherever you go in the world, always send your pictures in advance and place a call to your new market prior to departure. Also take with you all your most flattering and current pictures. Try to include editorial, catalogue, and character shots. Don't assume that you will know what the agent at the other end will like; I've sometimes found photos tucked away in the back of a book which I've liked more than those on display. If your book is weak but your look is strong, you can, of course, put your book together in your desired market, but this will cost more and delay your ability to work.

COMPOSITES

Comp-cards are much more problematic than portfolios. A card from Zurich, for example, may work well there, but agents in Italy may insist on having a new card for their market. Similarly, the Italian card may be unacceptable in Los Angeles, so yet another one has to be printed... This should not happen a lot, but it does happen. Each agent and market may have different approaches. When you have traveled a bit, you'll be better able to predict individual requirements.

WARDROBE

The best advice I can give is to wear lots of black: it tends to be the safest foundation for a "look," but be sure to inquire first.

TRAVEL DOCUMENTS

Obvious as it may sound, make sure you have a current passport. Jobs abroad can crop up at very short notice and it can take several weeks for a new passport to be processed. Don't miss out on work opportunities by being ill-prepared.

The visa/working paper situation varies from person to person, so it is very difficult to pin down. The information I give here applies only to American models and is current at the time of going to press. For up-to-date requirements, contact the agent before your arrival.

AIRPORTS

It can be rather unnerving the first time you arrive in a country and have to find your own way to the city center. For this reason I give the names of the major airport(s) serving each city and the approximate time it takes to get into town using taxis and/or public transport. Make sure you have some coins or small denomination notes for paying fares and tipping.

ACCOMMODATION

The type and availability of accommodation varies from city to city. If an agency has invited you to come, it will usually arrange some sort of housing. Most agencies have their own apartments which are less expensive to rent than private apartments. While this is convenient, remember that you will probably be sharing with one or more people. (I call it "dormitory life" because the population is so transient.)

If you're not already represented by an agency abroad, chances are that you won't be offered much help in finding accommodation. In this case the best thing to do is ask the advice of a model just returned from the relevant market. If you can't find someone, your agent will be able to help you.

TRANSPORT

Most cities have good public transport: subways, buses, taxis, bicycles . . . but there are cities where a car is essential. In the city breakdown, I specify which places this applies to.

PAYMENT AND COMMISSION

Payment schedules and commissions vary from agency to agency in Europe, while in the USA they tend to be the same for exclusive talent. Don't forget that some European governments take 20 percent (sometimes 25 percent) of your earnings (less than in the US).

LENGTH OF STAY

How long you stay in a particular city obviously depends on how well you are received, how much you like that market, and how much your agent believes in you. If you're doing well, you can extend your stay. If you're unhappy, you must talk to your agent there and plan an alternative strategy.

EXPENSES

This is a tricky area to advise about as the cost of living can vary enormously from place to place. If you're good at handling your money, obviously you'll fare better than those who aren't, but whatever your attitude to finances, do take care until you're working. Once you're reasonably established, you'll make friends who may offer to rent you a room in their apartment and this can be a real money-saver. The sums I quote for expenses include rent. These figures are estimates and intended only to give you some idea of what to expect.

Note that the information that follows is arranged alphabetically by country, and alphabetically within by city.

AUSTRALIA
MELBOURNE
Market Catalogue, advertising, and T.V. commercials. Consistent throughout year; slow in January and February. Limited minority market. Runway peaks in February and September.
Portfolio/composite Variety of images.
Wardrobe Neat, clean, fashionable; minimal make-up.
Documents Visa necessary.
Airport Tullamarine: about 20–30 minutes from city center by taxi or bus.
Accommodation $100 per week.
Transport Public.
Payment Every 2 weeks.
Commission 20%.
Length of stay 2 months minimum.
Expenses $1000 per month.

SYDNEY
Market Editorial, catalogue, advertising, and T.V. commercials. Work consistent throughout year, but relatively slow in January and February. Limited minority market. Runway peaks February/March and August/September.
Portfolio/composite Variety of editorial and catalogue.
Wardrobe Neat, clean, fashionable; natural make-up.
Documents Visa necessary.
Airport Mascot: 20–30 minutes from city center by bus or taxi.
Accommodation $130–$160 per week.
Transport Public.
Payment Every 2 weeks.
Commission 20%.
Length of stay 4 weeks minimum.
Expenses $1000 per month.

CANADA
MONTREAL, QUEBEC
Market Editorial with some catalogue and advertising. Peaks March through May, and September through November. Limited minority market. Runway peaks March, April, May, and September/October.
Portfolio/composite Editorial.
Wardrobe Clean, neat, and fashionable; natural make-up.
Documents Visa unnecessary.
Airports Mirabel: about 45 minutes from city center by regular bus service; about 40 minutes by taxi.
Dorval: about 20 minutes from city center by regular bus service, slightly less by taxi.
Accommodation $175 per week, $400 monthly.
Transport Public. Monthly bus/metro pass $43.
Payment Once a month.
Commission 20%.
Length of stay 2 months minimum.
Expenses $1000 per month.

TORONTO, ONTARIO
Market Catalogue, editorial, T.V., film, and advertising. Peaks February, March, and September. Slow during April, November, and December. Limited minority market. Runway peaks February and August.
Portfolio/composite Editorial with expression and spontaneity.
Wardrobe Casual, neat, fashionable; natural make-up.
Documents Visa unnecessary.
Airport Lester Pearson – about 40 minutes from city center by regular bus service, slightly less by taxi.
Accommodation $150 per week.
Transport Public. Monthly bus/subway pass $67.
Payment 1st and 15th of month; some only once a month.
Commission 20%.
Length of stay One month minimum.
Expenses $1000 per month.

FRANCE
PARIS
Market Primarily editorial with catalogue, T.V., film, and commercials. Busy year round, except August (all agencies close) and December. Limited minority market except for runway. *Haute couture* January and July; *prêt-à-porter* March and October.
Portfolio/composite Editorial.
Wardrobe Neat and fashionable; natural make-up.
Documents Visa necessary.

Greg Lotus

Airports/Aéroports Charles de Gaulle: about 40 minutes from city centre (Port Maillot) by bus or train (Gare du Nord). Orly: about 30 minutes by bus from city terminal at Invalides, or 20 minutes by train from Quai d'Orsay, Saint-Michel, or Austerlitz stations.
Accommodation $150–250 per week.
Transport Public.
Payment Varies.
Commission 25%.
Length of stay 2–3 months minimum.
Expenses $1000 per month.

GERMANY
HAMBURG
Market Editorial and catalogue. Peaks mid-March until mid-May, June, and September. Limited minority market. Very little runway.
Portfolio/composite Editorial with smiles.
Wardrobe Casual, fashionable: natural make-up.
Documents Visa necessary.
Airport/Flughafen Fehlsbuttel: about 30 minutes from city center by bus to Ohlsdorf station and then train, or 20 minutes by taxi.
Accommodation $150–200 per week.
Transport Public.
Payment Once a month.
Commission 20%.
Length of stay 2–3 months minimum.
Expenses $1200 per month.

MUNICH
Market Mostly catalogue with some editorial. Peaks January, March, and April. August very slow. Limited minority market. Very little runway.
Portfolio/composite Editorial with smiles.
Wardrobe Young, fresh, with some make-up.
Documents Visa necessary.
Airport/Flughafen Riem: about 20 minutes from city center; buses go to main railway station.
Accommodation $200 per week.
Transport Public.
Payment Once a month.
Commission 20%.
Length of stay 2–3 months minimum.
Expenses $1400 per month.

GREECE
ATHENS
Market Editorial, catalogue, and commercials; little runway. Work peaks from September to December and January to July. Dead at Christmas, New Year, and Easter.
Portfolio/composite Editorial.
Wardrobe Casual and fashionable; light make-up.
Documents Visa necessary, plus 6166 tax form from I.R.S.
Airport Glyfada: 20 minutes from city center.
Accommodation Hotels about $15 per night.
Transport Public.
Payment Dates vary from agency to agency.
Commission 30%.
Length of stay 50 days minimum.
Expenses $1000 per month.

ITALY
MILAN
Market Editorial with catalogue. Busy year round, except August (all agencies close) and December. Peak months are March, April, May, and June. Minority market for runway, otherwise limited. Runway peaks January and March, July and October.
Portfolio/composite Editorial.
Wardrobe Casual, fashionable, and natural.
Documents Visa necessary.
Airports/Aeroporto Linate: about 15 minutes by bus to the city's central station. Malpensa: about 40 minutes by bus to the city's central station.
Accommodation $175–200 per week.
Transport Public.
Payment Varies.
Commission 25%.
Length of stay 2–3 months minimum.
Expenses $1000 per month.

JAPAN
OSAKA

Market Catalogue, little editorial. Peaks May and June. Limited minority market. Little runway.

Portfolio/composite Editorial and catalogue.

Wardrobe Dressy to casual; lots of lingerie shoots.

Documents Working visa required The Japanese agency must invite the model to its market. It then sends a visa application to the model, who fills it out, takes it to the nearest Japanese consulate, and obtains a permit.

Airport Osaka International: about 30 minutes by road from city center (Osaka Station). Frequent taxis, buses, and trains; many agencies arrange pick-up.

Accommodation Agency provides apartment and advances the cost to model – about $350 per week.

Transport Agency rep drives models to first go-see and auditions. Thereafter, you must rely on public transport.

Payment Prior to departure, minus any advances for air fare, apartment, and allowances.

Commission 20–25% (+20% tax, total 40–45%).

Length of stay 2 months minimum.

Expenses Take little money; agencies provide an allowance (deducted from final payment). However, please be aware that Japan has a very high cost of living.

TOKYO

Market Catalogue, editorial, and runway. Slow during some holiday seasons (Christmas to New Year's Day, end of April to first week of May, and middle of August. Runway (including Tokyo Collection) peaks in April and October.

Portfolio/composite Fashion and editorial.

Wardrobe Stylish to casual; lots of sportswear and lingerie shoots.

Documents Working visa required The Japanese agency must invite the model to its market. It then sends a visa application to the model, who fills it out, takes it to the nearest Japanese consulate, and obtains a permit.

Airport Narita (New Tokyo) International: about 90 minutes from city center by taxi or bus: take airport shuttle bus to one of the international hotels, then take a taxi to the apartment or agency office since a taxi all the way from the airport is very expensive.

Accommodation Agency provides apartment and advances cost to the model – about £350 per week.

Transport Agency rep drives model to first go-sees and auditions. Thereafter, you must rely on public transport.

Payment Prior to departure, minus any advances for air fare, apartment, and allowances.

Commission 20–25% (+20% tax, total 40–45%).

Length of stay 2 months minimum.

Expenses Take little money; agencies provide an allowance (deducted from final payment). However, please be aware that Japan has a very high cost of living.

SOUTH AFRICA
JOHANNESBURG

Market Catalogue, advertising, commercials and T.V. Busy year round, with the exception of mid-December through mid-January. Lots of opportunities for minority models.

Portfolio/composite Editorial and catalogue.

Wardrobe Neat, clean, and fashionable: natural make-up.

Documents Visa and work permit necessary.

Airport/Aerpoort Jan Smuts: 20 minutes to the city.

Accommodation $250 per week.

Transport Public but very difficult.

Payment Varies.

Commission 20%.

Length of stay 3 months minimum.

Expenses $1000 per month.

SPAIN
BARCELONA

Market Catalogue, editorial, advertising, T.V., and commercials. Minority opportunities better than previously. Runway peaks February and September.

Michael McCafrey

Portfolio/composite Editorial with smiles.
Wardrobe Neat, clean, casual, fashionable.
Documents Visa unnecessary.
Airpor/Aeropuerto El Prat: about 15 minutes by taxi from city center, slightly longer by bus.
Accommodation $100–150 per week.
Transport Public.
Payment Varies.
Commission 20%.
Length of stay One month minimum.
Expenses $1000 per month.

MADRID

Market Editorial with some catalogue. Peaks in February through May. Slowest in August and December. Runway peaks February and September.
Portfolio/composite Editorial and catalogue.
Wardrobe Neat, clean, and fashionable.
Documents Visa necessary.
Airport/Aeropuerto Barajas: about 30 minutes by regular bus from underground terminal at Place de Colon.
Accommodation $100–150 per week.
Transport Public.
Payment Varies.
Commission 20%.
Length of stay One month minimum.
Expenses $1000 per month.

SWITZERLAND

ZURICH

Market Editorial, mostly catalogue. Peaks March, end August and end November. Limited minority market. Runway peaks March and September.
Portfolio/composite Editorial.
Wardrobe Neat, clean, and casual.
Documents Visa necessary.
Airport/Flughafen Kloten: about 10 minutes from the city center by bus, train, or taxi.
Accommodation $150 per week.
Transport Public.
Payment Varies.
Commission 25%.
Length of stay One month minimum.
Expenses $1000 per month.

UNITED KINGDOM

LONDON

Market Editorial, catalogue, advertising, T.V., and commercials. Peaks January and March. Runway peaks February, March, and October.
Portfolio/composite Editorial.
Wardrobe Casual and fashionable; natural make-up.

Documents Visa necessary.
Airports Heathrow: about one hour from city center (Piccadilly Circus) by subway or bus. Gatwick: about 40 minutes from city center (Victoria Station) by train.
Accommodation $100–150 per week.
Transport Public.
Payment Varies.
Commission 20%.
Length of stay One month minimum.
Expenses $1000 per month.

UNITED STATES

ATLANTA, GEORGIA

Market Catalogue, advertising, T.V., film, and commercials. Consistent through year; slow in December and January. Good minority market. Runway year round.
Portfolio/composite Editorial and catalogue.
Wardrobe Neat and casual; natural make-up.
Documents Visa unnecessary.
Airport Hartsfield: about 35 minutes from city center by shuttle bus, express bus or taxi.
Accommodation $100–150 per week.
Transport Car necessary.
Payment Varies.
Commission 20%.
Length of stay One week minimum.
Expenses $1000 per month.

CHICAGO, ILLINOIS

Market Catalogue, advertising, T.V., film, and commercials. Slow November through February. Peaks April through October. Runway peaks March and September. Excellent minority market.
Portfolio/composite Catalogue with some editorial.
Wardrobe Neat and casual; natural make-up.
Documents Visa unnecessary.
Airports O'Hare International: about 25 minutes from city center by taxi and about 40 minutes by subway (el line) or shuttle. Midway: (mainly domestic flights) about 30 minutes from city center by subway, bus, or taxi.
Accommodation $150 per week.
Transport Excellent public.
Payment Weekly.
Commission 20%
Length of stay One month minimum.
Expenses $1000 per month.

DALLAS, TEXAS

Market Catalogue. Consistent, but slow in April, May, and most of summer. Limited minority market. Runway peaks January, March, May, September and October.
Portfolio/composite Catalogue with some editorial.

Wardrobe Upmarket with natural make-up.
Documents Visa unnecessary.
Airport Dallas – Fort Worth: about one hour from center by shuttle bus (Surtran); about 30 minutes by taxi to central bus terminal.
Accommodation $150–175 per week.
Transport Car necessary.
Payment Weekly.
Commission 20%
Length of stay One month minimum.
Expenses $1000 per month.

LOS ANGELES, CALIFORNIA

Market Editorial, catalogue, T.V., film, and commercials. Busy year round, but slow in mid-summer. Good minority market. Runway peaks March through April, and September through October.
Portfolio/composite Editorial with smiles.
Wardrobe Casual; natural make-up.
Documents Visa unnecessary.
Airport Los Angeles International: about 45 minutes from city center by shuttle bus or taxi.
Accommodation $200 per week.
Transport Car necessary.
Payment Weekly.
Commission 20%.
Length of stay 1–2 months minimum.
Expenses $1500 per month.

MIAMI (SOUTH BEACH), FLORIDA

Market Catalogue, editorial, advertising, T.V., film, and commercials. Good minority market. Peaks late September through early March. Mainly a warm-climate location during winter. Very slow April through August.
Portfolio/composite Editorial and catalogue.
Wardrobe Very casual; minimal make-up.
Documents Visa unnecessary.
Airports Fort Lauderdale International: about one hour into central Miami by taxi. No shuttle available.
Miami International: about 30 minutes from city center by shuttle or taxi.
Accommodation $150–200 per week.
Transport Mainly by foot; car occasionally necessary.
Payment Varies.
Commission 20%.
Length of stay One month minimum.
Expenses $1000 per week.

NEW YORK CITY, NEW YORK

Market Editorial, catalogue, advertising, T.V., film, theater, and commercials. Peaks April/May through August/October. Good minority market. Runway peaks April, May, September, and October.
Portfolio/composite Editorial primarily.
Wardrobe Casual, neat, and fashionable.
Documents Visa unnecessary.
Airports John F. Kennedy (JFK): about one hour into city center (Grand Central Station) by shuttle bus or taxi. La Guardia: about 30 minutes into Grand Central Station by bus or taxi. Newark, New Jersey: not as far away as it sounds. Takes about 45 minutes by bus to terminal on 8th Avenue and West 41st Street.
Accommodation $150 per week.
Transport Public.
Payment Weekly.
Commission 20%.
Length of stay One month minimum.
Expenses $1200 per month.

PHOENIX, ARIZONA

Market Catalogue and some editorial. Peaks December, January, February, March, and April. Slow June, July, and August. All minority groups. Little runway; direct bookings. Rapidly growing market.
Portfolio/composite Editorial with smiles.
Wardrobe Clean, simple, fashionable; natural make-up.
Documents Visa unnecessary.
Airport Sky Harbor International: 15-20 minutes from Scottsdale by taxi or hotel shuttle.
Accommodation $300–450 per month
Transport Car.
Payment Every 2 weeks.
Commission 20%
Length of stay 1-3 months.
Expenses $1000–1200 per month.

SAN FRANCISCO, CALIFORNIA

Market Catalogue and some editorial. Busy year round, with the exception of May, August, and December. Good minority market. Runway peaks February, April, and August.
Portfolio/composite Editorial and catalogue.
Wardrobe Casual; natural make-up.
Documents Visa unnecessary.
Airport San Francisco International: 30–45 minutes from city center by shuttle.
Accommodation $175 per week.
Transport Public.
Payment 1st and 15th of month.
Commission 20%.
Length of stay 2 weeks minimum.
Expenses $1400 per month.

CHAPTER SEVEN

Roles and Tasks within the Industry

AGENCY

PHOTOGRAPHIC STUDIO

MODELING SCHOOLS

CONVENTIONS

CONSULTING COMPANIES AND SCOUTS

The world of modeling involves people in many different capacities. The important thing to remember is that all contribute to each other's success. The key word in modeling is "teamwork."

You must be aware by now that I love my job, but believe me, there are times when being an agent can be a thankless task. Most people are unaware of the pressures that agents are under, the responsibilities we have, the sacrifices we make, and just how much we are misjudged. Can you imagine being responsible for someone else's career, as well as your own? What about being responsible for several other careers, as well as your own?

Everything we do as agents affects our models' careers. We try with all our might to make sure the results are positive, but once in a while we make mistakes – and you should see the response! When we are making the models money and their schedules are busy, we're their best friends. They are happy and complimentary. Then, when there is a slight lull in the market, we promptly become the enemy and are held solely responsible for their schedules slowing down. Models never think that they too could be responsible, perhaps by being overweight, having skin problems, continually showing up late for bookings without their wardrobe, and so on. They're sure the agent is the only reason for their lack of bookings.

It's a tough business requiring enormous discipline. Imagine weeks of rejection – Monday morning comes with nothing scheduled. It would be much more comfortable to sleep until ten or eleven, but you have to get out there for your seven o'clock run and be ready for your agency by nine.

STAN MALINOWSKI Photographer

Modeling is a short-life career. It attracts young people who are given glamor, exposure, and rich rewards, and these things can go straight to their heads. Success and maturity do not necessarily walk hand-in-hand, and it's not unusual for models to turn against an agent who has nurtured their career and been instrumental in their success. As you might imagine, this is pretty upsetting for us. After working in the agency all day, taking clients to dinner, going to photo exhibits, socializing at parties, tracking down irresponsible models until late hours of the night, giving them a bed to sleep in, and expending our energies entirely on models' behalf, we really don't have much time to ourselves. As a matter of fact, private social life is non-existent. Everything we do somehow involves models or clients.

When I leave my work environment I forget that people don't know what I do for a living, and I frequently receive strange reactions. It's hard not to stare at attractive young men and women, appraising their appearance and wondering if they would make successful models. But other people have frequently misunderstood my interest and thought it must be sexual.

Every agent has many battle stories to tell, as well as the fairy tales. If you want to get a little personal insight into their lives, ask – that's if you really want to hear the truth!

AGENCY

The staff of a modeling agency can be many and varied: owners/agents, bookers, administrators, secretaries, book-keepers. Administrators generally "manage" the office. The owner/agent and/or booker generally "manage" the models' schedules and careers. The scout is a talent-hunter who travels around the world looking for new talent and placing existing talent. This job can be held by an agency staff-member, or a freelance person working either for a specific agency or for all agencies, being partial to none.

It's fascinating to watch a busy agency. If you're not in the business, it can look like a madhouse of chaos and confusion. A well-run agency functions like a well-oiled machine – it just seems like a crazy environment. This is not to say that it's not full of stress and pressure. But if the employees all like each other, they laugh through the dramas and traumas of their day. Trying to get into the flow of the agency is like driving down a quiet country road on a Sunday afternoon and then hitting a highway ramp; if you don't know how to merge into the traffic, you could sit for hours waiting for attention.

When I became a booker, I answered the telephones, wrote and typed my own correspondence, edited all the female film, laid out all the portfolios, interviewed all the aspiring models, photographers, make-up artists, hairdressers and clothing stylists, scheduled all the female models', hairdressers' and make-up artists' appointments, arranged their tests, cleaned the office... I was a jack of all trades, filling the roles of administrator, agent, scout, and booker. It was not uncommon for me to leave the office at 10:00 P.M. only to return promptly the next day at 9:00 A.M. In fact, I got more work done after regular office hours, when I wasn't dealing with moment-to-moment emergencies.

Now that I am co-owner of my own agency, I pretty much handle all the above-mentioned duties for female fashion models. Thankfully, I now have an amazing staff who help me to get it all done. While I'm handling Aria daily duties, I'm also working on special projects such as writing/updating this book. On occasion I actually sneak away from the insanity to go to my favorite workout – shidokan karate. When I return to the office in the early evening, I have completely forgotten about the stress of the day and finish my work.

Photographic Studio

Each professional has an individual style. As you learn more about the different types of model and the various markets, you will also learn more about the different types of professional and their styles. They all work together. The key is to find the people who have the right style for you and also appreciate your look.

Just as every person has a unique personality, so he or she also has different degrees of talent, different business ethics and practices. It is difficult to describe the "typical" photographer, photo agent, photo assistant, hairdresser, make-up artist, clothing stylist, or art director. Some people have never had any formal training. They began by picking a career, jumping in, and learning by trial and error. Some may start with a little school training, others may have a college degree.

Talent does not necessarily always make a person successful. Politics also has a significant influence in our industry, just like any other. I know of many talented people who do not work often; I also know of people who are not considered to be talented who work a lot. Studios can be hotbeds of intrigue, so never gossip or be indiscreet. Even casual remarks, such as, "I went to a really good party last night," will be reported back and used against you if anything goes wrong. Those shadows under your eyes in the finished photograph may be the photographer's fault, but the blame will be laid at your door if you talk too freely about your outside activities.

Try to feel positive about working with your chosen professionals, particularly at the beginning of your career. They should talk you through the photo session, explaining every step so that you understand what is required of you for that specific job. If you are uncomfortable or dislike any of them, those feelings will be read on the film.

Some people are extremely difficult to understand. Don't be alarmed – there is considerable responsibility resting on their shoulders to produce a first-rate product. For example, you might begin your day with a nit-picking, highly strung, over-sensitive photographer who by the end of the day could be low-key, carefree, and prepared to compromise. It is important that you try to understand the pressure these people are under. Don't label them or lump them into any kind of category – they are all different, just as models are. And

Friends have sent girls my way who they thought would be wonderful models. Often they are highly attractive, but most lack that indefinable quality which distinguishes a great model from the common. Of course, these girls become confused and disappointed when they see a seemingly less attractive girl move past them to the pinnacle of modeling success.

Stan Malinowski Photographer

always remember: the more effort you make, the better relationships you will have with your co-workers, and the smoother your transition from "aspiring" to "professional" model will be.

In many ways, the photo studio functions like a modeling agency. Each member of staff, regardless of number, works together as a team. I don't believe models truly understand the pressures, responsibilities, and power that each position has to handle. The following breakdown is to give you insight.

Photographer

The photographer is instrumental in developing a model's look. Certain photographers have the ability to see a special quality in a model which may have been overlooked by others. It is the photographer's responsibility to capture the model's unique presence on film. Photography is an art form: the photographer is the artist, the model is the subject and the film is the canvas.

Have you ever visited an art museum? Perhaps you have noticed that what some people admire, you absolutely hate – and vice versa. Viewing pictures is a subjective exercise and no two people will have exactly the same opinion. This is precisely what happens with models. Some people will appreciate your look and some will not. You must try to look at yourself unemotionally and judge your photographs as a whole. It is very difficult at the beginning of your career to distinguish between good and bad photography. Until you develop an "eye" you should rely on your agent's suggestions.

Photographer's assistant

The photo assistant is responsible for anything involving camera equipment. The basic qualification for the job is a good knowledge of photography. (Do you remember the character Radar in the TV series *M.A.S.H.*? Remember how he was there at the Colonel's side before the Colonel even knew he needed him? Well, that's exactly how a good photo assistant should be.) The assistant rarely leaves the photographer's side. If he does, he returns before the photographer misses him. An assistant is usually an employee of the photographer, but may sometimes operate on a freelance basis. This position is usually the lowest paid of any in the photo business.

MAKE-UP ARTIST

Studio make-up artists are responsible for making up the models. They may be qualified beauticians or simply have a natural flair for make-up and skin care. They can be employees of the photographer or studio, represented by an agency, or freelance. (See Chapter 3 for more information on make-up.)

HAIRDRESSER

A studio hairdresser is responsible for styling models' hair. He or she will normally be trained in cutting, coloring, perming, and all the other necessary techniques, and can give the new model good advice on hair care outside the studio. The hairdresser can be an employee of the photographer or studio, represented by an agency, or freelance. (See Chapter 3 for more information about hair.)

CLOTHING STYLIST

As the title suggests, the stylist is responsible for the clothing at a photo session. This person will prepare the clothing provided by the client, ironing it and sewing buttons and hems if necessary. She also scouts for clothing, accessories, and props that will enhance a photo

session. The stylist is responsible for acquiring the items, maintaining their condition, and returning them to their proper place. Stylists are often clothing designers. While a knowledge of photography can be helpful, it is most important to have a great sense of fashion, the ability to move quickly and to work very long hours (before and after each photo session, as well as during it). The stylist can be an employee of the photographer or studio, represented by an agency, or freelance.

PHOTOGRAPHER'S REPRESENTATIVE

A photo rep represents the photographer in much the same way as a modeling agent represents a model: he or she sells the photographer's services. The rep must have a knowledge of photography and the photographer's capabilities, and be a good hustler. Reps frequently hold go-sees on the photographer's behalf, making a preliminary selection of faces from which the photographer will make a shortlist. This saves time and keeps a busy photographer up to date with new faces on the market. Most reps are freelance and represent more than one photographer, which means they deal with many different areas of photography. They normally take a percentage from each job they get the photographer.

It's so frustrating sometimes when you take a shoot seriously — working so hard, putting in so much time and energy to ensure that the end product is absolutely incredible — and someone you've hired comes in with a bad attitude and doesn't care about the product or you. It makes such a difference when you're working with a professional who takes their work and yours seriously.

LINDA THOMSEN
Photographer's Representative

ART DIRECTOR

This person can be of vital importance to models, as the art director is the client — the person employing the

Marie Anderson Boyd

◀ *The hairdresser and make-up artist discuss the model's make-up while the photographer's assistant organizes the male models.*

Marie Anderson Boyd

Many times I have preconceived ideas as to how I'm going to style a specific model. Then they walk into the room and their disposition, gestures, body movement, and stance will often give me a different direction to go in.

LEE ANN PERRY Clothing Stylist

photographer and other people involved in the photo session, and art directs the shoot. Back at the office he then produces the advertisement. In fashion advertising this means the page is laid out (designed), copy (text) is written and typeset, photos are sized, keylining is organized and finished. When the art director approves, the page is sent for the buyer's approval. Finally the ad goes to press.

If the ad is not approved, there have to be reshoots. There could be many reasons for this: maybe the visual presentation doesn't show the merchandise favorably; it could even be that the store has sold out of the merchandise. If reshoots are necessary, it reflects badly on the art director – more expense will be incurred, and going over the budget puts his or her job in jeopardy. Is it any wonder that art directors tend to be anxious at photo sessions?

photographer and all the staff involved in a shoot. Some art directors are freelance, but most work for a specific store or advertising agency. In retail art direction, an art director could be working on six projects in an hour; in advertising art direction, the pace is much slower – perhaps one project over six months. The art director has to be highly creative while also being responsible for production of the shoot, staying within the budget, meeting the deadline, satisfying his employers, and keeping the buyers and their bosses happy. The art director is the person who conceives the idea, books the

Using their knowledge and discretion, Art Directors make split second decisions with long term impact on their clients' images.

ROY SKILLICORN Executive Producer

🔺 ▷ *A photo shoot is normally a hive of activity, with each member of the team collaborating to produce the best possible photos. Here you can see a male model working with the clothing stylists.*

Marie Anderson Boyd

MODELING SCHOOLS

You will hear many conflicting opinions about modeling schools/self-development centers. I feel that a good one can be of incredible assistance in teaching the basic requirements, as well as providing network potential for a modeling career. Some schools even have agencies attached to them, so aspiring models can gain local experience before moving on to a more competitive market.

Are modeling schools absolutely necessary? No — but when I take on well-trained models, we can all make money faster because they are already clued up about the business. For example, they have decent haircuts, they move well, and have photos that I can use in Chicago.

I believe agents should explain why we do or don't want to represent you; usually, there's a specific reason. If you're rejected, perhaps you need to lose weight, clear up bad skin, develop a better attitude about dedicating yourself to modeling, or find some more money to invest in your career. Whatever the reason, a good school director can help you make the necessary changes, then liaise with agents when you're better prepared. I'm delighted to send commission checks to schools who send me well-prepared potential models; those who waste my time simply lose my business.

Never be pretentious or inconsiderate, and always remember that there is a fine line between being grateful and being ingratiating.

JIM STREACKER
Senior Art Director

If you are interested in attending a modeling school, visit several and examine what each has to offer. Do they have outdated model photos on the wall? Are the photos of their own models or simply torn from magazines? Listen to what people are saying. Are they discussing last year's fashion news? Do they have the furry eyebrows and long nails of the 1970's? Ask questions. What major international agencies do they work with? What models have they placed recently with those agencies? How many of those models were successful? Review their curriculum. Sit in on a class, if they'll allow it. Check the Better Business Bureau: do they have lots of complaints about them?

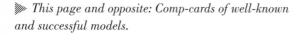 *This page and opposite: Comp-cards of well-known and successful models.*

▲ *Tony Bruce's comp-card.*

▲ *Yasmeen Ghauri's comp-card.*

Jerry Brody

CYNTHIA CRAWFORD

Height: 5'9"	Bust: 34B	Hair: Lt. Brown
Weight: 116	Waist: 22	Eyes: Brown
Dress: 5-6	Hips: 34	Shoe: 8½

TALENT MANAGEMENT CORPORATION
STEWART

◢ *Cindy Crawford's first comp-card.*

François Mathys

PAUL SCULFOR

◢ *Paul Sculfor's comp-card.*

If possible, take an adult with you for moral support and to deter unscrupulous operators from trying to cheat you. Above all, use your common sense and heed your instincts. If something doesn't feel right, it's probably inappropriate for you.

SCOUTING CONVENTIONS

Modeling conventions are gatherings at which agents, fashion scouts, and aspiring models can meet and assess each other. They are usually held over a weekend and charge an admission fee, but they are an efficient and relatively inexpensive way of meeting people from many different markets, both home and abroad.

A typical convention, which may attract hundreds of people, offers seminars and other activities to impart basic skills to aspiring models. You then have the opportunity to walk down a runway in front of all the participating agents and scouts. Each candidate carries a number and those whose numbers are called out are invited for personal interviews with the agents; the others are asked to leave.

Don't be put off if you are rejected – at least you tried, and maybe next time you'll be more confident. Those who get "call-backs" usually have a hurried interview with one or more agents, but there's no guarantee that you'll be taken on. For most newcomers, conventions are just a step in the right direction.

> *Conventions are an excellent way to be discovered. Models learn how the business works and see if they have what it takes.*
>
> DAVID VANDO   Models Mart

CONSULTING COMPANIES AND SCOUTS

The main task of modeling consultancies is to advise aspiring models and then try to place them with a top agency. They charge the models for the consultation, and if they are successful in placing them, they then receive a commission from the agency. Scouts acting independently don't normally charge aspiring models: they receive a commission from the committed agency.

Good consulting and scouting companies can save agents a great deal of time. In fact, I interview many of the models they send me and I've made many signings.

If you're thinking of contacting such a company, check out several to be certain you're dealing with reputable people.

Nutrition and Exercise

The secret of looking good depends as much on what you eat as what you wear. Good nutritional habits will help you cope with the stress and strain of a demanding job.

NUTRITION BY ERIC HOFFMANN

Like it or not, modeling is a career that is often influenced by other people, but nutrition and exercise are two areas over which you can take control. What you eat will not only affect your performance and appearance, but your personality and attitude as well. A balanced diet can give your skin a healthy glow, put shine in your hair and a special brightness in your eyes, as well as enhance your mental alertness and stamina.

FACTS ABOUT FOOD

The nutrients in food provide energy, encourage growth, and are essential for the healthy maintenance of our bodies. Foods can be divided into three categories: carbohydrates, fats, and proteins. It is important to understand the role of each nutrient in order to achieve a properly balanced and varied diet.

CARBOHYDRATES

Carbohydrates are energy foods. During digestion, they are converted into glucose – sugar which is circulated in the blood, providing the body with its primary source of energy. When not used immediately, glucose is stored in the liver and muscles. There are two types of carbohydrates: simple and complex.

Simple carbohydrates (simple sugars) are found primarily in fruits, fruit juices, and sweet processed foods, such as cakes and sweets. As these are rapidly released into the system, the body may experience a burst of energy after eating them, but this is soon followed by an energy depletion. More significantly, the quick release and absorption process means that simple sugars are readily converted into body fat. Also, as most processed simple carbohydrates lack essential vitamins, minerals, and fibre, they're not a great bonus in your diet.

Complex carbohydrates are found in whole grains, beans, vegetables, breads, and pasta. Thanks to their complex molecular structures, more time and energy are needed for these carbohydrates to be absorbed and utilized by the body, so less is needed in order to feel full. In addition, the glucose obtained from complex carbohydrates supplies more nutrients than simple carbohydrates, so it also provides more sustained energy levels. Always drink plenty of water when consuming large amounts of fibre since these carbohydrates may be stored as fat if consumed in excess. It is recommended that 60 percent of our daily food intake should consist of complex carbohydrates, so try to limit your processed food intake and opt for more natural foods.

PROTEINS

Protein is present in every cell of our bodies and is essential for the growth and maintenance of all human tissue. As the body is constructed of protein and is in an ongoing state of growth and repair, it needs protein from food to maintain it. Protein is also essential during exercise, when muscle tissue is broken down and then rebuilt. It also helps the body to produce antibodies, which fight disease and strengthen the immune system. A daily diet of 15–20 percent protein is adequate for most people, but those with a very active lifestyle may need more. The best choice of protein is a high-quality "complete protein" – one that supplies all the essential amino acids. Egg whites, fish, white poultry meat (such as chicken and turkey) and lean cuts of red meat (such as sirloin steak and filet mignon) are excellent choices. Although grains and vegetables also contain protein, they typically lack or are low in some essential amino acids. Baking, broiling, grilling, and poaching are the healthiest ways to prepare these foods. Again, lots of water (8–10 glasses daily) is recommended.

FATS

Fat serves several important functions in the body. Not only is it the largest potential source of energy, but it also aids in the absorption of certain vitamins, protects cell membranes, and is used in the production of certain hormones which regulate nearly every system in the body. Monounsaturated and polyunsaturated fats (jointly referred to as unsaturated) are found in avocados, nuts, some cold-water fish, vegetable oils, and olive oil. Saturated fats derive from animals and are found in meat, poultry, and dairy products. Our bodies, too, can manufacture saturated fats.

Unsaturated fats contain essential fatty acids (EFAs), which the body does not produce, so they must be obtained through food. When EFAs are in good supply, our bodies function better, skin and hair retain a healthy glow, and our immune systems are stronger. Conversely, it has been well documented that saturated fats consumed in large quantities promote the build-up of cholesterol, which may clog up the arteries and eventually lead to disease.

Most of us consume too much fat in our daily diet. The current recommendation is to consume no more than 30 percent fat, preferably less, with saturated fat limited to 10 percent. When you shop for food, read the labels, where the nutritional information is all spelled out, and opt for unsaturated fats whenever you can.

CALCIUM

Some 99 percent of the body's calcium supply is needed for the teeth and bones. However, for the calcium to be absorbed by the body, adequate levels of vitamins C and D must be available. Calcium absorption tends to decline with age, leaving the body to draw on calcium deposits in the bones. This can lead to osteoporosis (brittle bones), a condition which is much more common in women than men. Consumption of too many soft drinks or too much meat (and thus, too much phosphorus) may also increase the need for calcium. To ensure an adequate intake of calcium, make dairy products, canned salmon, and/or dark green vegetables a part of your daily diet.

VITAMIN SUPPLEMENTS

Vitamins are organic compounds that perform essential functions for good health and normal body maintenance and development. The body does not make vitamins but obtains them from plants and from animals that consume plants. If you follow a sensible and varied diet, vitamin supplements are generally not needed. To minimize vitamin loss, cook fruits and vegetables quickly, limiting the time they are exposed to heat; better yet, eat them raw.

IRON

Iron is carried in the blood and is vital for good health. Insufficient levels of iron cause red blood cells to become small and pale, a condition known as anemia. Iron deficiency can cause loss of appetite, fatigue and reduce resistance to infection. Due to blood loss during menstruation, iron deficiency is more common among women. Good sources of iron are lean red meat, liver, leafy green vegetables, kidney beans, and wholegrain bread. Take care to eat foods rich in vitamin C to enhance iron absorption from plant sources and to limit absorption inhibitors, such as coffee.

WATER

More than three-quarters of the body is made up of water. In fact, water is so important to all bodily functions that we cannot survive more than a few days without it: dehydration begins in just a few hours. The body loses approximately 3 pints of water per day, so make sure you drink 7–10 glasses of water to replace it. Fruits and vegetables contain between 60 and 95 percent water, so they will also aid in water replacement. Water is great for the skin and for cleansing the system, and it has exactly 0 calories. Note that alcohol, tea, coffee, and cola act as diuretics, making you urinate more frequently and thus increasing the need for additional water.

FOOD LABELING

Government regulations insist on detailed food labeling, so it is easy for consumers to tell exactly what they are eating. As ingredients are listed in order by amount, with those at the top of the list making up most of the product, try to avoid processed foods that list sugar within the first few ingredients. Watch out too for ingredients ending in -ose, such as glucose and fructose, as these are sugars and should be regarded in the same way as refined white sugar. Foods which are least processed and low-to-moderate in saturated fats, sugars, and sodium are the wisest choices.

EATING DISORDERS

Modeling is a business that calls for lean and healthy good looks in both men and women, and it is all too easy to let preoccupations with weight and imposed misconceptions of beauty dominate your life. It is wise to devise a sensible nutrition and exercise program and avoid any faddish or unhealthy diets.

Unfortunately, some models develop a compulsion to be thin, going to extreme lengths to achieve their goals. This may involve periods of starvation (anorexia) or periods of heavy eating (bulimia), followed by purging with laxatives or self-induced vomiting. Not only is this damaging to your body, but such regimes do nothing for your looks, and may eventually jeopardize your career. Eating disorders are not simple conditions; they can lead to serious health problems and even death. If you suffer from any of these, talk to a doctor or nutritionist who can help you to sort things out.

BALANCING YOUR DIET

The body needs many different nutrients to remain healthy, so it is essential to eat a variety of foods every day. One of the easiest ways of ensuring a balanced intake is to eat at least the minimum recommended daily servings

FOOD GROUPS	SUGGESTED DAILY SERVINGS
Group 1 Breads, cereals, rice, pasta, wholegrain products	6-11 per day
Group 2 Fruit – apples, oranges, melons, berries, grapes, etc.	2-4 per day
Group 3 Vegetables – dark green leafy, deep yellow, dried beans and peas (legumes)	3-5 per day
Group 4 Meat, poultry, fish, eggs, beans, seeds, nuts	2-3 per day
Group 5 Dairy – milk, cheese, yoghurt	2-3 per day (men); 3-4 per day (women); 4 per day (teenagers)

Menu Plans

The menu plans below and on page 145 are based on the food groups outlined on the previous page. The first block has been devised for meat-eaters, the second for vegetarians. Both offer a minimum intake of 1500 calories. The right-hand column has additional and/or alternative items which may be included to bring the daily intake up to 2000 calories.

MEAT-EATERS' MENU	
1500 calories	**Additions/alternatives for 2000 calories**
Breakfast	
• 2oz bran cereal	
• $\frac{1}{2}$ 9-inch banana	
• 1 slice rye toast	
• 1 cup low-fat or skim milk	
Lunch	
• 1 cup split pea soup	3 small crackers
• 1 slice wholewheat bread	
• 2oz roast chicken	
• 1 tsp mayonnaise	
• 2 lettuce leaves	
• 2 slices tomato	
• 1 apple	
• 1 cup low-fat or skim milk	
Supper	
• 3oz lean steak, grilled	2 small boiled potatoes
• 1 wholewheat roll	1 tsp margarine
• 2oz steamed broccoli	$\frac{1}{3}$ 5-inch melon
• 1oz mozzarella cheese	
• 1 small boiled potato	
• 1 cup tea with lemon	
Snacks	
• $\frac{3}{4}$ fresh pineapple	1 cup non-fat yoghurt
	4oz fresh strawberries

VEGETARIAN MENU

1500 calories	Additions/alternatives for 2000 calories
Breakfast • 2oz/ bran cereal • ½ 9-inch banana • 1 slice raisin bread • 1 tsp margarine • 1 cup low-fat or skim milk	2 slices wholewheat toast 2 tsp margarine
Lunch • 3oz wholewheat pasta • ¾ cup fresh tomato sauce • 2 tsp Parmesan cheese • 5 grapes • mineral water	3oz salad 2 tsp oil and vinegar dressing 15 grapes coffee, tea or water 3 small crackers
Supper • 1 cup split pea soup • 3oz spinach salad topped with 1 medium sliced orange • 2 tsp low-calorie dressing • 1 small pumpernickel roll • 1 cup low-fat or skim milk • 3 ginger snaps	2 wholewheat rolls 1 fresh peach
Snacks • 1 cup non-fat yoghurt • 4oz blueberries	1 medium apple chopped into yoghurt 2 tsp raisins

EXERCISE BY CURTIS BRACKENBURY

Modeling is a business that demands élite physical characteristics. Your body is your livelihood, a fact you must always keep in mind. Success comes about through a combination of factors, but the most important is preparation. Perhaps you will be an overnight sensation, or maybe you will have to slog every step of the way. Whatever the case, preparation will lay the foundation for the future. It will enable you to stay healthy and maintain a steady income for a long period of time.

Wherever you go, no matter what continent, everyone talks about health and fitness. In Milan, Paris, New York, London, and Tokyo the philosophy is the same: eat right, work out, look great. But first of all you must ask yourself some questions. What is right for me? What is right for my career?

PREPARING AN EXERCISE PLAN

Preparation involves taking a long, hard look at yourself, noting and highlighting your strengths, identifying and improving your weaknesses. In order to make this assessment, you need to consider the following things.

FUNDAMENTAL QUALITIES OF A MODEL
Whatever market you specialize in, good posture is a vital attribute in modeling. It must be combined with fluid body movements and good balance, both of which can be achieved by sensible exercise programs.

WORKLOAD
A model must know when particular markets are busiest so he or she can balance work and exercise demands efficiently. During intense periods of modeling your priority is work – exercise plays a lesser role. When work is quieter, exercise comes to the fore, giving you the opportunity to prepare your body for specific markets.

TIME
Using your time efficiently and realistically is important. You must establish a schedule which allows you to complete your normal daily activities without overstretching yourself.

CLIENT DEMAND AND RESPONSE
Feedback from the people you work for is extremely valuable. It can give you an insight to your market, help you identify what the client likes and dislikes, and thus help you be better prepared. When you have examined each of these things and know what your time and temperament will allow you to do, you must take a long hard look at your body. Keeping your body in shape and in demand requires attention to three main things:

1 POSTURE
It is a common complaint among clients and photographers that too many models have poor posture: round shoulders, sway backs, and small bulging stomachs. Designers and clients want models who will enhance their products, so you must practice holding yourself properly to eradicate these defects. Look at the photo below to see an example of good posture.

2 BALANCE
Professional models make it look easy, but spinning and twirling in front of cameras and bright lights, perhaps while wearing high heels or climbing stairs, is quite a skill. They mustn't "cheat" by using their arms for balance or looking at the ground – they must move instinctively and learn to "feel" where they are at all times. It requires constant practice to achieve good balance – to move naturally and easily without apparent regard for the surroundings. One step on the way to achieving this is to acquire muscular strength so that you have greater control over your movements.

▶ *Good posture.*

John Beckett

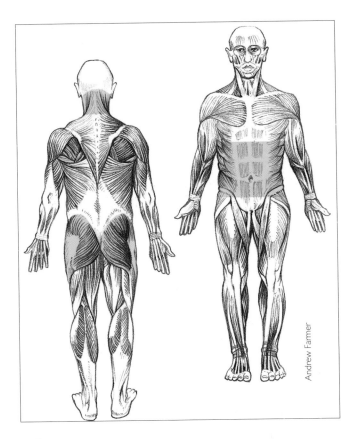

▲ *The "core" muscles.*

Whether you've just started your career in modeling or have years of experience, the benefits of proper nutrition and exercise will assist you not only in reaching your career goals but in living a more complete and healthy life.

ERIC HOFFMANN

shaded areas control posture. It is most important to move the core muscles in a slow, controlled fashion.

Outlined on the following pages is a sequence of exercises which will help you to build up your muscles. For all the exercises, the points below always apply:

- Do all exercises slowly.

- Do all exercises in the full range of motion (i.e. extending yourself as far as you feel comfortable).

- Do each exercise in three stages:

  1 Lift up for a 4-second count

  2 Pause for 4 seconds

  3 Lower for a 4-second count.

- Stop at once if something hurts.

- Do not hold your breath.

- Count out loud while exercising – it will help you to breathe naturally.

- Each time you do an exercise, it is called a "repetition." Slowly build up your strength until you can complete 10 repetitions.

- 10 repetitions are called a "set." Your eventual goal is to complete 3–5 sets.

- Each side of the body is exercised separately. When you have completed one set of each exercise, change positions and work on the other side of the body.

- Remember that "form" is most important. Do not try to increase your range of action by moving other body parts. If your muscles cannot manage something, don't do it. As your strength increases, so will your range of flexibility.

3 MUSCLE STRENGTH

Modeling often calls for movements to be repeated or for poses to be held for long periods. Apart from stamina, you will need good muscle control to make the movements graceful and smooth. Make a mental note of the sort of poses required in a standard modeling session and practice them at home. Stand in front of a full-length mirror, lift your arms, then let them drop to your sides. Now exert some real muscle control by lifting them again slowly and pausing halfway up for five seconds. Bring them back down slowly. Repeat this exercise with your legs and head. Concentrate on improving the movements that you find awkward or jerky. Remember, you may have to hold or repeat certain movements all day in a modeling session, so you must build up the muscle strength to perform as well at the end of a shoot as you did at the beginning.

In order to increase your strength, improve your posture, and develop fluid movement patterns you must follow an exercise program. First of all you must work on body stability which is controlled by the "core." As you can see from the illustration, the core is a large area controlling the arms, legs, and neck. The muscles in the

In the first week or so of your exercise program, the aim is to make your body "aware." Try to do approximately 3 sets of exercises with 5 repetitions per set. Then progress to 3–5 sets of 10 repetitions 3 times per week.

CORE EXERCISES

STARTING POSITION FOR NECK BENDS

1 Kneel on the floor, placing the hands on the floor 15 inches in front of the knees.

2 Keep the abdominal muscles tight and the pelvis tucked towards the back.

3 Keep the back straight and the eyes fixed on the ground.

4 Tuck the chin into the chest.

BACKWARD NECK BENDS

1 Adopt the starting position.

2 Slowly, on a 4-second count, keeping the shoulders steady, roll the head back.

3 Pause for 4 seconds.

4 Return to the starting position on a 4-second count. (Don't forget to count out loud.)

FORWARD NECK BENDS

1 Adopt the starting position.

2 Slowly, on a 4-second count, keeping the shoulders steady, roll the head forward.

3 Pause for 4 seconds at the end of your range of motion.

4 Return to the starting position on a 4-second count.

SIDE NECK BENDS

1 Adopt the starting position.

2 Slowly, on a 4-second count, move your head to one side and try to touch your shoulder with your ear. Do not change your form.

3 Pause for 4 seconds at the terminal point.

4 Return to the starting position on a 4-second count.

5 Repeat the exercise on the other side.

NECK TURNS

1 Adopt the starting position.

2 Slowly, on a 4-second count, turn the head 90 degrees to the left.

3 Pause for 4 seconds.

4 Return to the starting position on a 4-second count.

5 Slowly, on a 4-second count, turn the head 90 degrees to the right.

6 Pause for 4 seconds.

7 Return to the starting position on a 4-second count.

BODY SIDE BENDS

1 Lie on your right side on the floor.

2 Secure your feet.

3 Tuck in your chin, keep your shoulders back, hold in your abdominal muscles, and keep your buttocks tight.

4 Place your right arm across your chest.

5 Keep your left arm resting on the side of your body.

◀ *Experienced models move with grace and agility, even under the most demanding conditions. Walking, dancing, and twirling along the runway in front of a large and critical audience is not easy, but you can make it look easy when you have good muscle control.*

▲ *Body side bends.*

John Beckett

6 On a count of 4, lift the upper body and slide the left arm towards your knee.

7 Pause for 4 seconds in a position within your range of motion that allows you to keep your form and control. As your strength increases, you will be able to get closer to your knee.

8 Return to the starting position on a count of 4.

9 Repeat the exercise on the other side.

Remember not to go past the point of control in any exercise.

SIT-UPS

These exercises are designed to create strong abdominal muscles which hold in the stomach and strengthen the lower back, helping to prevent lower back pain. They are graded from 1–3 in order of difficulty, so you should start with the easiest and work your way up. As you "curl up" the upper back and shoulders, remember to push the abdominal muscles toward the floor. Do not secure your feet. On the return portion of the exercise, imagine the backbone being lowered inch by inch so that you have complete control.

STARTING POSITION FOR SIT-UPS

1 Lie flat on the floor.

2 Bend the knees approximately 90 degrees.

3 Tuck in the chin.

4 Tilt the pelvis towards the chest.

5 Push the abdominal muscles towards the floor.

LEVEL 1 SIT-UPS

1 Adopt the starting position.

2 Place your hands on your thighs.

3 Roll your head towards your chest.

4 Roll your shoulders forward, sliding your hands gently towards your knees.

5 On a count of 4, curl the upper body to the point where the lower back is just about to rise.

6 Hold this position for 4 seconds.

7 On a count of 4, return slowly to the starting position, lowering the vertebrae one by one.

LEVEL 2 SIT-UPS

1 Adopt the starting position.

2 Place your hands across your chest.

3 Roll your head and shoulders forward.

4 Repeat steps 5–7 of level 1.

LEVEL 3 SIT-UPS

1 Adopt the starting position.

2 Place your hands behind your head.

3 Roll your head and shoulders forward.

4 Repeat steps 5–7 of level 1.

This concludes the core exercises. Now it is time to use that stabilizing strength and develop balance and fluid body movement. The following exercises will give you a feeling of motion and control.

BEAM EXERCISES

The beam is a great and inexpensive way to enhance your modeling career. Get a length of 4 x 4-inch wood which is at least 6 feet long. (You may find it easier to get wood which is 2 inches thick; if so, buy two lengths and nail them together.) Before you start work on the beam, sandpaper the wood so there is no danger of splinters. Place the beam on the floor and you're ready to start.

THE FORM

It is essential to adopt the correct posture for beam exercises: keep the back of the neck long and the chin drawn in; "pinch" the shoulder blades together, then lower them gently to keep shoulders back; pull the chest down and in by using the upper abdominals. Tighten the lower abdominals as if you want them to touch your back. Finally, clench the muscles in your buttocks. It will help if you can practice in front of a mirror, then you can see what the correct form looks like. As you become more familiar with the exercises, your body will feel more comfortable.

THE FIRST STEP

The toes are the first part to touch the beam; they should be used in a sensitive, gripping fashion. The heel is next; it should be lowered gently. To check your leg position look down: the knee should be in a straight line with the inside of the toe. The other foot is placed comfortably behind the heel of the foot in front. You may feel the foot moving in and out, trying to balance. This shakiness will decrease as the strength in your stabilizer muscles increases. Now, looking straight ahead, take a step forward as follows. Push the pelvis forward, shifting the weight on to the balls of your feet. Then swing the back leg forward and start the process again. Keep looking straight ahead at all times. Your hands and arms should be at your sides in a controlled but relaxed manner.

LEARNING TO BALANCE

It is important not to watch your feet or to worry about what is happening down below. The aim is to "feel and sense" what is happening. If you find it difficult to balance, turn your thumbs outward as far as they can go. If you feel yourself swaying to one side, don't flap your arms around to gain your balance. Try to correct your

Balance in life is important. In the modeling industry, physical balance is an irreplaceable essential. How well you walk, pivot, bend, or pace depends on your sense of balance, and an excellent way to sharpen your sense of balance is to improve flexibility.

EDDIE YOSHIMURA Karate Sensei

1

2

3

position by using the "core" muscles. For example, if you are swaying to the right, tighten up the muscles on the left side of the core. While all this is going on, don't forget your posture. It is important to maintain the correct "form" at all times.

MOVING ON THE BEAM

Whether moving backwards or forwards on the beam, steps should always be taken in the same way: lead with the pelvis, feel with the toes, then lower the heel. When you get to the end of the beam, stop. Lift both heels, then pivot 180 degrees and face the other way. If the right leg is ahead, turn to your left; if the left leg is ahead, turn to your right. If you want to move sideways, the weight has to be transferred to the balls of the feet because the beam is narrow. Always maintain your form. If you lose control, stop, collect yourself, and start again.

Tackle the following exercises in the sequence given. By working through them slowly and methodically you will acquire the muscle strength to achieve good balance and control. You might like to start by practicing them on the floor. Once you feel comfortable, move to the beam.

LEVEL 1 BEAM

1   Adopt the correct form.

2   Step on to the beam, looking straight ahead.

3   Walk slowly to the end of the beam.

4   Stop, then return backwards along the beam.

LEVEL 2 BEAM

1   Adopt the correct form.

2   Step on to the beam looking straight ahead.

3   Lift up on your toes one foot at a time, then both feet together.

4   Make slow, controlled pivot turns, first to the left, then to the right.

5   Gradually build up speed.

6   Hop on one foot, then the other.

7   Stand sideways on the beam.

8   Slide feet sideways along the beam.

LEVEL 3 BEAM

1   Adopt the correct form.

2   Stand sideways on the beam.

3   Cross the right leg over the left

4   Bend and touch the beam with the left hand.

5   Repeat, crossing the left leg over the right.

6   Bend and touch the beam with the right hand.

7   Lift one leg and hold for 5 seconds.

8   Lift one leg and lower the body as far as you can without losing your form.

9   Hold for 5 seconds, counting out loud.

4

5

1   *The correct "form" on the beam.*

2   *Walking along the beam.*

3   *Moving sideways along the beam.*

4   *Lifting one leg on the beam.*

5   *Catching a ball without losing balance or form.*

John Beckett

ADVANCED BEAM WORK

- Try doing all the previous exercises with your eyes closed. Really try to feel and sense where you are at all times.

- Ask somebody to throw you a ball. Try to catch it without moving your head and losing your form. Follow the ball with your eyes. This ability will stand you in good stead for fashion shows and camera work.

Now you are ready to start doing some serious training on the beam. The following movements are designed specifically for models.

HALF TURN

1   Stand on the beam with the right foot forward. Most of your weight should be on the back foot.

2   Step forward, transferring the weight on to the ball of the right foot.

3   Twist your upper body to the desired direction and pivot on the ball of the right foot.

4   As you near completion of the turn, gently place the toes of the left foot on the beam.

5   Transfer your weight to the left foot while the right foot is prepared either in a stance position or is ready to walk out of the turn.

HIP MOVEMENT

1   Walk along the beam, keeping the upper core and shoulders steady while moving the hips.

2   Then walk along the beam keeping the hips steady while practicing shoulder movements. Remember, walking on the runway requires the shoulders to be tilted slightly back.

3   Once you get control, practice moving the hips and shoulders at the same time.

WALKING

Practice walking along the beam on the balls of your feet. This helps you to move well when wearing high heels.

STANDING

Photographic work requires two kinds of strength: one allows you to stand motionless for long periods of time, the other allows you to move gracefully. Sometimes you may even be required to hold bizarre positions, such as standing on one leg with arms stretched out. Have a look at current fashion magazines and see how the models are posing. Then practice on the beam in front of a mirror until you are strong and graceful.

1   Stand on your right foot.

2   Bend the knee and hold the left foot 2 inches off the beam in front of the body to a count of 4.

3   Gradually raise the foot until it is 12 inches off the beam to a count of 4.

4   Finally, raise the foot until it is 24 inches off the beam to a count of 4.

Once you can do 3 sets of 10 repetitions, increase the holding time progressively to 30 seconds, then to 1 minute.

John Beckett

▶ *Energetic dancing can be a good alternative way of keeping supple.*

◀◀ *Half turn.*

◀ *Walking on the balls of the feet.*

Michael McCaffrey

FLEXIBILITY

The goal of being or becoming flexible is to improve your overall range of motion. The following is a proven method to achieve just that: all you need is a little space.

- *What should you do? Develop a routine. Stretching can range from a quick five minutes to an hour, depending on your schedule and how motivated you are.*
- *When? Before you go to sleep, on waking up, when traveling, on the beach...*
  - *Where? Anywhere there's space.*

- *Why? Besides improving your sense of balance, stretching also relaxes you, both physically and mentally, improves your mind–body coordination, and reduces your chances of injury, muscular cramps, strains or tearing.*

- *How? The key to flexibility is relaxation, and the key to relaxation is proper breathing. Inhale for a count of 4, exhale for a count of 7. Think of it as a form of "active meditation." Stretch slowly and deliberately. Make it a part of your daily routine and you will be surprised at the results.*

EDDIE YOSHIMURA Karate Sensei

Handling Your Finances

Wise money management is a critical factor in a successful, long-term career, so it is important to set aside time in order to organize your finances. Sifting through your receipts and invoices on a regular basis will help prevent a once-yearly filing nightmare.

TAX CONSIDERATIONS FOR SELF-EMPLOYED MODELS

Originally written by Debra Lessin, this chapter has been updated by John J. Ayotte for U.S. models, and by Françoise Allaire and Allen Church for Canadian models. (Please note that, for simplicity, the accountant is referred to as "he" throughout.)

Being a model requires a lot more than a pretty face. It is extremely important to organize yourself sensibly and be responsible for your money. This chapter offers you general guidance about handling your finances, but as the industry becomes more global and the tax laws more complicated, it is in no way sufficient to replace a personal accountant. Please do not take this area lightly. Many models who have not paid their taxes have ended up in very serious trouble. Any time you make or spend money, it must be accounted for.

WHAT IT MEANS TO BE SELF-EMPLOYED

Your relationship with the modeling agency or agencies that represent you is that of an "independent contractor." For employment and tax purposes, you are responsible for keeping track of your income and expenses, providing for your own employee benefits, i.e. health insurance, disability insurance, social security taxes, retirement, etc. and for calculating and paying your own income taxes.

When you are self-employed, the burden for paying social security tax (self-employment taxes) rests solely on you. In a more traditional employer/employee relationship, the employer pays one half of the social security taxes, and the employee pays the other half. These taxes deducted by an employer would be listed as "Fica" and "Medicare fica" on your pay stubs.

As an independent contractor, taxes are not withheld from the income you receive. Generally you are required to pay quarterly estimates to the Internal Revenue Service (I.R.S.) and to your local taxing state. These quarterly taxes must be paid currently in the year you are working. For example, taxes for 1997 would be due and payable as follows:

April 15, 1997
June 15, 1997
September 15, 1997
January 15, 1998

In Canada, models must also calculate and remit their taxes on a quarterly basis, the dates for which are the 15th of each March, June, September, and December in every year. In many cases, Canada Revenue will advise you as to how much your instalments should be.

It is extremely important that you set aside enough cash from your income to properly remit the quarterly taxes that are due. All too often, models come to us several years in arrears and do not have the money to pay the taxes due. Your accountant can help you determine how much to set aside for quarterly tax payments, and can provide the necessary quarterly tax vouchers to remit payments.

Income, social security, and state income taxes are payable on your *net* modeling or acting income, i.e. all the money you have left after all your expenses have been deducted. Below is a broad overview of the various tax rates:

Federal income taxes	15–39.5%
Self-employment (social security taxes)	15.3%
State and local taxes	0–12%

AGENT'S FEES

While you may think that you work for your agent, the reality is that your agent works for you. *Webster's Dictionary* defines an agent as "one who acts for or in the place of another by authority from him." Your agent acts for you in promoting you and arranging bookings in your behalf.

An agent's resources, experience, and staff all have a price tag. A commission is paid on the monies you earn through his professional efforts. Commission percentages vary from agency to agency and from city to city. The industry norm is 15 or 20 percent. One of the services your agent provides is to bill clients for your bookings and collect payment. Upon settlement, your agency will send you a check for the booking fee less their commission.

Your check may also include deductions for any business expenses you have incurred if you have asked your agency to pay them on your behalf. These expenses may also include some general promotional costs, such as headsheet expenses, which are arranged by the agency on behalf of you and the other models they represent. Organizing payment of such expenses is an administrataive burden for the agency, as well as a cash flow drain. Business expenses are really your responsibility – unless, of course, the client agrees to cover them as part of the booking agreement.

Deductions for cash advances and the agency's commission will generally be the *only* deductions from your check. Taxes will *not* be deducted because you are not considered to be an employee of your agency. You are self-employed. Your agency merely facilitates your billing, collection, and promotional activities.

As soon as you begin your modeling career, find yourself a Certified Public Accountant (C.P.A.), or a Chartered Accountant (C.A.) in Canada. Financial horror stories abound about models who neglect the financial: they incur heavy penalties for late payment of tax, non-payment of estimated tax, and late filings of tax returns. There is also compound interest due on the tax owed. You can avoid such penalties and the horrible hole they leave in your pocket if you hire a good accountant from the outset.

CHOOSING AN ACCOUNTANT

It is important to find an accountant with the C.P.A. designation because there are many accountants and tax preparers in business today who do not keep up with the constantly changing tax laws. An accountant who has earned the educational and professional credentials to obtain the C.P.A. designation *must* keep abreast of tax laws in order to maintain a license.

Finding someone who simply knows the tax laws, however, is not enough – your accountant should also be familiar with the modeling business. Unless he understands the nature of the industry, you can be sure that certain deductions or items pertinent to your taxes will be overlooked.

While you must take overall responsibility for record-keeping and documentation, your accountant should guide you about what is and is not important. He should spend time discussing your career with you and finding out how you keep track of your income and expenses. He should then help design a

Marie Anderson Boyd

Scott Chambers

simple and functional record-keeping system for you that can be easily used on a regular basis. Nothing complicated is required. However, you must accept that you will have to do some paperwork if you want to be a successful model. Without this you cannot prove that you have spent money for business-related expenses. The end result: you pay more in taxes. Perish the thought!

Technical expertise aside, perhaps the most important facet of the relationship with your accountant is trust. Are you comfortable with your accountant as a person? Does he make himself available to answer your questions or take your calls? Does he communicate with clients on a regular basis in an understandable manner, be it by phone, letter, or in person? Apart from keeping abreast of tax laws, does your accountant also provide you with tax-planning options and opportunities? Does he tell you in simple terms what you need to know and do? Does he anticipate the questions you have and pro-actively communicate suggestions? Does he have the resources and business network to direct you to people who can help you invest your money when that day eventually comes?

Too often people fear their accountants. In the long run, that fear will result in an unsatisfying relationship. Whatever preconceived notions you have about

accountants, it is possible to find some who care about people and who communicate with their clients in English, not "accountantese!" You want someone who enjoys working with people in a one-to-one professional relationship and who believes his function is to save the clients' money. The numbers become secondary – it's the people who matter. How do you find such a person? Ask your fellow models for recommendations. The best testimonial an accountant can ever get is a satisfied client.

KEEPING TRACK OF INCOME

We recommend that you open a separate checking account in which to deposit the income you receive from modeling or acting. The deposits you make into this account will generally represent the income you earn as an independent contrctor. It would also be a good idea to keep a "cash receipts" journal listing all the deposits you make into the account, and verifying that the journal you keep agrees with the deposits made to the bank. Copies of the deposit slips should be kept in an appropriately labeled envelope.

At the end of a calendar year, you should receive a Form 1099 for each of the agencies you worked for if your earnings exceeded $600. You should compare these 1099's to your records to verify that the agency has accurately reported your income both to you and to the I.R.S.

KEEPING TRACK OF EXPENSES

It is perfectly possible to achieve financial success and independence in the modeling industry, but when you start your career you may well find that your outgoing cash exceeds your income. Among the out-of-pocket business expenses you will incur are prints and composites, cosmetics, taxis, air fares, hotels, and so forth. You need to keep track of each and every expense in an organized manner on a consistent basis.

Sometimes it can be hard to distinguish between a personal and a business expense, particularly when your physical self is so much a part of your business. However, once you learn the fine distinctions, be sure to keep track of all relevant expenses. In fact, it's advisable to keep track of everything you spend your money on, just in case you need to itemize it later. Your accountant can evaluate the significance of each expense in relation to your business.

If you don't keep track of your expenses, you will pay taxes on the gross income paid to you through your agency. This does not benefit you financially because that overpaid tax money belongs in your pocket, helping you to build a secure financial future.

We recommend that, whenever possible, business expenses be paid either on a dedicated business charge card, or by writing a check from the separate business account you set up to deposit your income.

A simple way to keep track of out-of-pocket expenses is by using the "envelope method." Start off by buying seventeen large envelopes and a file box to keep them in. Next, in the upper left-hand corner of each envelope, write the year and expense category. Categories applicable to your business include the following:

Deductible Expenses
- Accounting fees
- Agency fees or commissions
- Cosmetics
- Dues and publications
- Educational seminars, training, coaching
- Entertainment
- Equipment (e.g. fax machine)
- Postage and courier expenses
- Gifts (less than $25 per person)
- Grooming (hair, nails, etc.)
- Miscellaneous office expenses and supplies
- Motor expenses
- Prints, composites, portfolio costs
- Taxis and public transportation
- Telephone
- Travel – air fares and local transportation
        hotels and lodging
        car rental
        meals
- Wardrobe

Now that you have your envelopes and an idea of the specific categories, you can begin to use them. Whenever you incur a particular expense, place the receipt in the appropriate envelope. If you don't obtain a receipt for some reason, you need to keep a written note of the expense. For example, you may tend to forget small, out-of-pocket expenses such as taxis, but over a period of time, these expenses add up. At the end of every day in every week, sort out your receipts and place them in the appropriate envelope.

If you keep up your records on a regular basis, it will become a habit and save you the cumbersome task of organizing your receipts at the end of the year. Documentation is undoubtedly the key to lowering your tax liability and is a valuable safeguard against the day when the I.R.S. might choose to audit your tax return. While an audit is always an unnerving experience, even your accountant's mind will be easier if your records are organized and well documented.

Occasionally, you will need to add some more specific information on the face of a receipt to indicate its relevance to your business. Examples relating to specific expenses are described below in the section on tax-deductible expenses: some relate to information required by law for tax reporting purposes; others relate to certain expenses specific to the modeling industry.

TAX DEDUCTIONS

AGENCY FEES AND COMMISSIONS
The fees and commissions you pay your agency qualify as deductible business expenses. In addition, other pass-through expenses are allowable as deductions

ENTERTAINING
Entertainment of "business associates" may be deductible if your guests can be reasonably expected to engage or deal in the active conduct of your business. Meals, sporting event tickets, and nightclubs are

Scott Chambers

examples of expenses that qualify as entertainment expenses. Currently, 50 percent of the cost of business entertainment is allowed as a deduction.

To substantiate these expenses you must keep track of the "who, when, where, and why" relating to the entertainment. You must be able to supply the following documentation in support of business entertainment:

• The person you entertained, and their occupation and business relationship to you.
• The date the entertainment took place.
• The place, including address, where the entertainment took place.
• The reason for entertaining, and the benefit expected to be derived from the entertainment.

Wherever possible, use your charge card to pay for entertainment as the time and place are recorded on the payment slip. Write the name of the person entertained and the reason for it on the back of the slip.

MOTOR

Expenses for automobile usage are deductible either under a standard mileage allowance, or by specifically computing the actual operating costs of a car. In most circumstances, the standard mileage rate is the most practical method of keeping track of your automobile expenses. For 1996 the standard rate is 31 cents per mile.

You should keep track of your auto mileage on a daily basis. The best place to do this is in your diary next to the relevant booking or appointment. If you prefer, you can compile this information in an auto log book (available from office supply stores) and keep it in the glove box of your car.

TRAVEL

Sometimes modeling work may necessitate traveling to other cities for bookings, interviews, go-sees, or merely to experience another market. As these away from home expenses are directly related to your business, they are allowable as deductions.

Air fares and transportation costs are deductible regardless of the duration of the trip. Meals are deductible only if the trip requires an overnight stay. They may then be deducted either on a *per diem* (daily) rate, or on an actual costs incurred basis.

Expenses incurred as a result of a long-term assignment may be deductible as travel exenses. These may include apartment rental, utilities, car rental, meals, etc. Generally, the out-of-town assignment must be one year or less in duration, and you must maintain your original primary residence.

WARDROBE

Contrary to common belief, a model's entire wardrobe is not a deductible business expense. Clothing that is adaptable and wearable as ordinary apparel at non-working times may not be deducted. However, clothing purchased specifically for an engagement, and not suitable for everyday wear, is deductible. Dry cleaning and care of clothing specifically for a booking are also allowable expenses.

FOREIGN TAXES

The treatment of income earned from foreign sources differs, depending on how long your employment out of the country lasts. Since most bookings abroad are less than 365 continuous days, discussion here is restricted to travel abroad lasting for less than one year.

First and foremost, your expenses incurred abroad qualify as travel expenses. The examples cited earlier for long-term assignments also apply to foreign travel. Generally, your gross income earned while abroad is subject to tax withholding by the foreign country in which you work. However, you will not usually file a tax return in that country. All income earned by you, including foreign and domestic income, is reported to the I.R.S. on your return to the United States. To prevent the inequity of paying taxes twice on this income, the I.R.S. allows you to take either a tax credit or a tax deduction for the foreign taxes withheld. You can choose whichever method is most favorable. Generally, it is advisable to keep separate records of money earned abroad and money earned in the United States.

Withholding tax is also deducted from payment which arises from work performed in Canada.

Models who are Canadian residents will generally be taxable in Canada on their income earned from engagements anywhere in the world. They may also be taxable in the foreign country in which their services are rendered, although this tax will generally reduce their Canadian tax liability. Once again, it is important to discuss this with your personal accountant.

WORKING IN CANADA

Foreign models (including Americans) need a working visa to work in Canada. If you do not have a specific booking, a good way to find out if it is worth while obtaining the requisite papers is to visit a few agencies to learn about opportunities in the Canadian market.

Taxes are not deducted from a foreign model's income, although the agency's fee and the regular promotion and logging expenses are withheld where applicable. Models are paid by check and may cash it directly at the agency's bank upon presentation of acceptable identification. When the model leaves Canada, the remaining funds can be taken as a bank draft or certified check, both of which are accepted in most foreign countries.

Foreign resident models who are considered to be self-employed will be taxable in Canada on their income earned in Canada, net of related expenses. The Canadian tax will generally be available to reduce tax in their home country. In some cases, the terms of Canada's tax treaties may exempt models from Canadian tax altogether.

CONCLUSION

By now you should have a broad idea of the tax rules and regulations that apply to the modeling profession.

The process of accumulating your tax records does not begin when you sit down to prepare your tax return. The process of record-keeping begins the day you begin your career as a model. Tax planning is only effective when the deductions and record-keeping requirements are anticipated in advance, rather than reconstructed after the year has ended.

Early in your career, seek out a C.P.A. who can thoroughly explain the complex tax rules as they relate to the modeling industry. You need a professional who can help you prepare and plan early in the process. You should find someone who will aid in planning and managing your income tax costs and burdens rather than someone who merely assembles your tax return from data you have provided.

If you become successful in your chosen career, it is likely that your combined income tax expenses will be one of the largest expenditures you make. It is imperative that you lawfully use the tax rules and regulations to your fullest advantage.

All the information given here may seem rather overwhelming, but it can only benefit you in the long run, providing security for you now and in the future. As your career progresses, financial planning may become even more vital. Although it may seem a long way off, the day *will* come when you will want to consider various retirement plan options available for self-employed individuals.

Modeling should be fun, but it should also provide you with tangible financial rewards. It is a business and you must always remember to treat it as such. This way you will be more aware of your financial responsibilities to the government and to yourself.

CHAPTER TEN

Commercial Acting

GETTING A FOOT IN THE DOOR

COMMERCIAL ACTING OPPORTUNITIES

TRAINING

GLOSSY AND RÉSUMÉ

Acting classes do far more than simply teach you how to act. They also help you to develop confidence and poise, two vital attributes that will aid your career, no matter what direction you finally choose to pursue.

As you've probably realized by now, modeling is a short-life career, so you need to be thinking of what your experience equips you for come the day that you "retire." This section deals with the transition from fashion modeling to commercial acting, a path that many former models pursue. Perhaps you can even think of some models who have made the transition successfully – Lauren Hutton, Cybill Shepherd, Kim Basinger....

In the following pages I outline the concept of commercial acting, make you aware of the (normally unmentioned) resistance you will meet from the acting community, and advise you on the organization of your glossy and résumé. There are many books and classes which can give you detailed direction on how to pursue an acting career. This section merely aims to help you decide if acting holds any interest for you. If it does, be prepared! In the beginning, models-turned-actors are disliked by the acting industry, so they must work extremely hard to earn the professional actor's respect.

Fashion agencies send headsheets to all casting directors and agents as those people are constantly looking for new faces. When they call us, we are peppered with questions about specific models: Where are they from? Can they work in the U.S.? Do they have regional accents? Do they have any training? Can they handle copy yet? It's imperative that they learn if they wish to compete on a professional level.

MICHAEL BAIRD   TV and Film Agent

GETTING A FOOT IN THE DOOR

Commercial acting is one of the easiest areas for a model to get into, but few people in the acting world believe that modeling is a suitable background for anything other than modeling. Actors tend to think that models acquire acting jobs based upon their looks rather than talent or any special skills. Ask any seasoned actors how they feel about models becoming actors and you'll get some pretty strong reactions, often resentful and cynical. Many of these actors might have been struggling for years – moonlighting as waiters or waitresses, taking interminable classes and going on endless auditions – only to lose countless jobs to new, young whipper-snappers who may be more attractive. Naturally, they become disheartened.

Even though models may not come into the modeling world with the head and heart of an actor, they should at least learn commercial acting technique so that they can handle a piece of copy, speak well on camera, and audition.

MICHAEL BAIRD
TV and Film Agent

Ask casting agents how much they expect to get from a model in a casting session and they have have high hopes. Hoever, they are often let down by models who have not bothered to find out what a commercial casting or audition requires. This sloppy approach creates many hours of frustration and irritation for casting agents; it is not their responsibility to teach models how to audition. Is it any wonder that models have a reputation for laziness and stupidity?

These harsh facts are intended to give you some insight so you will be better prepared to handle any discomfort that comes your way. If you wish to be accepted and respected, you must play by the industry rules. Be sensitive and understanding of the acting community, and the rough road ahead will be more tolerable for everyone.

Models should know that if they can really act, every door is opened to them.

TERRY BERLAND   Casting Director

COMMERCIAL ACTING OPPORTUNITIES

There are two types of commercials which frequently cast models. Non-air commercials are those not intended for broadcast use, such as non-broadcast audience reaction commercials, copy testing, or client demos. Photomatics are one specific type of client demo – they use a still photographer and the images are converted to video using special techniques to give the feeling of movement, as in ordinary film. This type of commercial is less expensive and faster to produce than a moving commercial. Non-air commercials give new actor/models a chance to see what it takes to produce a commercial and provide valuable experience to add to acting résumés.

The second type of commercial involves real movement, and may have speaking or non-speaking parts. Models cast for this type of commercial may find themselves modeling clothes, advertising a store, selling a mattress, buying a car, opening a bank account, eating an ice cream – you name it!

Speaking parts usually require voice training. Clients frequently request models who can speak as well as act, but very often they'll cast for the model's looks alone. If the model looks right, but is inarticulate or has a regional accent, dubbing or looping will be necessary. For example, a Kentucky accent might alienate customers in New York, so the model will mouth the words during filming and an acceptable voice-over will be dubbed on the soundtrack after filming. Be warned – having a regional accent will severely limit your speaking parts. Voice training will be necessary if you are serious about your acting career.

In both photomatics and ordinary commercials, parts are available for principals and extras.

A principal part is the position held by the featured actor in a commercial. That actor is the representative of the product the consumer will focus on, and the part may be either speaking or non-speaking.

Extra parts, which may be speaking or non-speaking, are held by people who are strategically placed to fill unwanted space in a commercial. Never underestimate the importance of these parts; an extra can always be upgraded. Being an extra is a terrific opportunity to learn the inside workings of commercial production without the stress of being a principal. It allows you to observe what is required of the principal actors, the creative process involved, and the roles of the production team. Always grasp any opportunity to learn something new – it could bring you that bit nearer to your goal.

TRAINING

Regardless of what country or market the commercials you wish to audition for are aimed at, you must have proper training. As I became more experienced as a print agent, I wanted to learn more about the commercial acting business, so I took an on-camera commercial acting class. It took eight weeks and was an incredible learning experience. It's amazing to learn things that the professionals make look so simple: how to handle a product so that the consumer can read it; timing the copy (words) while handling the product; learning how to bite into a hamburger (there are specific classes available to teach people the art of eating on camera). You'll also learn techniques for psyching yourself up for auditions and overcoming intimidating directors. The amount of training that you require will become obvious as you get involved in the business.

Randy Kirby is a successful model-turned-actor who regularly appears in commercials and even gives seminars about commercial acting all over the United States. He talked to me about his experiences and attitudes toward his work.

"Acting in T.V. commercials is lots of fun. It can also be very demanding – doing take after take until it is exactly right. To me, it's an art form, just like photography. My advice to aspiring actors is strive to be the very best you can, and always be looking for ways to improve."

While commercial acting can be a regular and lucrative source of income (particularly with repeat fees), you might begin to aspire to "higher things." If you develop serious theatrical ambitions, for example, you would be well advised to undertake proper training at a reputable drama school. It is rare to find a theatre professional who gives much credit for commercial acting experience. It just isn't in the same league.

As a former fashion print booker and current on-camera agent for T.V. and film, Carrie Johnson has insight into the transition between modeling and acting. "As an agent, I face many obstacles when I try to push casting directors to see my model-turned-actors. The simple fact is that models are not taken as seriously as classically trained actors, and as a result they must work even harder to gain respect."

"My advice to any model who wants to act is to immerse themselves into classes. This is not a short term commitment of taking just one class; you need many. A cold-reading class is beneficial because copy is often not available before an audition. I also urge my models to take improvisation acting classes. These teach you how to be free, less inhibited, and not afraid to do something silly. Finally, get a monologue under way and audition for theatre."

"Models need to separate the two worlds of acting and modeling. Use your composite for modeling and your headshot and résumé for acting. A high fashion photographer would not book someone for a major print campaign on an actor's headshot nor would a casting director cast a major job solely on a model composite. However, what you can bring from modeling is to transfer the feelings and emotions you exude on a print shoot to an audition. Many models feel as if they are acting or creating characters when they model which may help you get into character when auditioning."

"Be professional and come prepared to an audition. This means to be on time, know your lines, wear the appropriate clothing, listen, take direction, and be self confident."

"If you treat acting like a business and treat it with the same enthusiasm and drive you do modeling, success should surely follow. Best of luck!"

▶ *Although in Britain you can use your model's portfolio and comp-card for acting interviews, actor-models in the United States should use a black-and-white head shot (otherwise known as a "glossy") along with a written résumé of their work. This shows that they are serious about the acting profession, and not just models.*

Renee Maria

KEITH COUSINO

Actors' head shots above, as distinct from models' comp-cards shown below.

RENEE MARIA

KEITH COUSINO

▶ *Elizabeth Hickling, actress turned model turned actress.*

GLOSSY AND RÉSUMÉ

The acting world's equivalent of a portfolio is a good black and white head shot and a professionally laid out résumé. A fashion model's composite will not suffice for a commercial client. You must adhere to the acting industry requirements if you wish to be accepted and appreciated. Before you invest any money in your acting career, you should first consult an acting agent. Most modeling agencies have film divisions or affiliated agencies that handle all their acting requirements. If you are fortunate enough to be a model with a print agency which has a film associate, your transition from modeling to acting will be easier.

A glossy is a black and white photograph measuring 8 x 10 inches, showing your head and part of your shoulders. Your first and last names are normally printed below the photo. You eyes should be level with the camera. Avoid tilting your head or shrugging your shoulders. This type of body language can suggest indecision or insecurity. You are selling a product, so it is necessary to look like a sales person – decisive and confident! (You may see character actors who have silly photos; this does not apply to models.)

Your character, attitude, wardrobe, make-up, and hairstyle should all be consistent with the image that you want to project. Avoid loud fabrics and distracting jewelry. Keep it clean and simple. Avoid any "fashion model" influence. Remember that you are appealing to the mass public, so maintain the "commercial" concept.

A résumé is a one-page, typewritten history of your related experience. It should be the same size as your glossy as it is stapled to the back of it, printed side out. It should have details of you and your agency, and clearly list your accomplishments over no more than the previous two or three years. A typical order of listing might read as follows: name, height, weight, unions, agency, appropriate education and training, theater, film, and commercial experience, special skills (including foreign languages), talents, and finally, your

It can be frightening for models to reach the age of thirty and find themselves at the beginning of their career again. If they've made some preparations, though, it can be a very exciting time.

ELIZABETH HICKLING   Actress and Model

special interests. Do not include any kind of modeling experience and for security reasons, do not include your address, phone number or social security number. The advice given here is only for your general guidance. Your agent will assist you in preparing your résumé.

Every country has its own rules and regulations. Always ask about the commercial acting opportunities and requirements whenever you travel abroad. It's possible that the experience and training you have in one market may not be appreciated in another. For example, commercials you have made in Japan may not be acceptable to European clients. You may have to take classes for a particular market as it's crucial to understand each market's culture and its consumers. The more you travel, the easier it will become to adapt.

AUTHOR

MARIE ANDERSON BOYD

Marie has been in the model management field since 1979, beginning at the age of twenty. She has worked as a studio manager for international fashion photographer Stan Malinowski and as an agent for Elite model agency in Chicago, where she was promoted to Vice President after seven successful years. She is now co-owner of Aria Model and Talent Management in Chicago.

Marie is married and lives in Chicago with her husband, Cortland. She spends her free time pursuing her hobby, shidokan karate, under her sensei, Eddie Yoshimura. This is the second edition of her highly successful book.

Modeling Information
from Aria Model & Talent Management Ltd.
1.900 988 8888
$3.00/minute – average 5-8 minutes a call
Monday – Friday 10:00 a.m. – 4:00 p.m. Central Standard Time
Must be 18 years of age
Aria Model & Talent Management Ltd., Chicago, Illinois
Customer Service 312 243 9400

Chris VandeGuchte

CONTRIBUTORS

MAUREEN BURKE

Maureen has been a professional make-up artist since 1981. Originally trained in cosmetics at Vidal Sassoon in Chicago, she currently resides in southern California, from where she promotes her own line of cosmetics, M. Burke Maquillage. She continues to work in the fashion industry for editorial, catalogue, and advertising shoots, and also works in the film industry on music videos and commercials. Her work has been seen internationally in a variety of magazines, including *Vogue*, *Allure*, and *Marie Claire*.

Jennifer Meltzer

GARY NOVIT

Gary Novit has been a senior stylist at the Vidal Sassoon Salon in Chicago since 1983. His experience with the modeling business includes haircutting and styling for major fashion shows and magazine shoots throughout the world. Gary also does hair for national advertisements and T.V. commercials, including those for Vidal Sassoon.

Jerry Avenaim

CLANCEY CALLAWAY

Clancey is an expert in color and texture. Part of the Sassoon organization since 1985, she was recently appointed the North American Head of Chemical Department, and works out of the Chicago salon. In addition to a very heavy client load, Clancey is responsible for Vidal Sassoon's chemical training across the country, and works regularly with the top magazines.

Mark Lind

DAVID LOVE

As Men's Director of Look Model and Talent Management in San Francisco, David has developed and managed the careers of many international models. He considers that his success in the industry is due to his having been both a model and a booker. David graduated from the University of Michigan with a B.A. in Psychology.

Thomaf Krappitz

ERIC HOFFMANN

Eric has been a competitive athlete since 1975. He has an undergraduate degree in Liberal Arts and a graduate degree in Business Administration. He is a certified personal trainer and an international model and actor. Eric learned about diet and nutrition through extensive studies, as well as his years of practical application on himself and his clients. He is confident that his lean, hard appearance enhances his performance and marketability as a model. He maintains 6–7 percent body fat through exercise and proper nutrition.

Oleg

CURTIS BRACKENBURY

John Curtis Brackenbury is President of Prime Corporation, a consulting company monitoring the principle of efficiency in physical fitness. True to his ideals, Curtis is enviably fit, having played professional hockey for eleven years, completed the Iron Man Triathlon in Hawaii, and interned at the Institute of Sports in Australia. He currently lectures and designs fitness programs for Aria models.

JOHN J. AYOTTE

John J. Ayotte has a B.S. in accounting, and a Master of Science degree in taxation. He is president of Ayotte & Samonds, Ltd., a firm which provides accounting and financial advice for individuals and businesses. They have extensive experience working with independent contractors, including models, actors, actresses, dancers, and others in the performing arts.

ACKNOWLEDGEMENTS

The author and publishers would particularly like to thank the following people and agencies for their help:

Françoise Allaire, Guido Argentini, Jerry Avenaim, Michael Baird, Neal Barr, John Beckett, Fadil Berisha, Terry Berland, Tom Bien, Gerard Bisignano, Mary Boncher, Allan Boyd, Jerry Brody, Maureen Burke, Brenda Burns, Dr Richard Caleel, Clancey Callaway, Mark Cameron, Regan Cameron, Ashley Carman, James Caulfield, Peter Chadwick, Scott Chambers, Allen Church, Michael Colliander, Rita Craig, Ashli Degenford, Tony D'Orio, Terry David Drew, Anthony Edwin, Paul Elledge, Elo, Bridget Etzkorn, Aldo Fallai, Andrew Farmer, Mike Felder, Paul David Fisher, Kevin Fry, Marjorie Graham, Guzman, Shirley Hamilton, Peter Han, Marc Hauser, Christopher Hawker, Liz Hickling, Eric Hoffmann, Beth Hyatt, Interesting Development Photography, Robert Jaso, Carrie Johnson, Susanne Johnson, Paul K., Matt King, Jim Kirchman, Thomaf Krappitz, Blair Kruse, Andrew Lamb, Lillian Laureano, Mark Lind, Matthew Lipton, Greg Lotus, David Love, Donald MacPherson, Stan Malinowski, Matthew, François Mathys, Michael McCafrey, Peter McClafferty, Leah McCloskey, Brian McConkey, Rod McNeil, Jennifer Meltzer, Peter Modler, Wolfgang Mustain, Kathy Nedved, Gary Novit, Ann O'Malley, Oleg, Olick, Lee Ann Perry, Paul Rackley, Huggy Ragnarsson, Michael Ramion, Rodney Ray, Michael Roberts, Norman Jean Roy, Russell/Rutheford, Drew Riker, Sebastian, Stewart Shining, Roy Skillicorn, Carter Smith, Johnathon Glynn Smith, Pedro Spoggi, Dale Stackler, John Strange, Jim Streacker, Donna Surges-Tatum, Scott Teitler, Rick Thomas, Linda Thomsen, Chris VandeGuchte, David Vando, Vanessa Victor, Michael Voltattorni, Ellen Von Unwerth, Paul Wadina, Bruce Weber, John Welzenbach, Andi Westerman, Alexandra Winner, Winston, Cela Wise, Stephen Wolter, Eddie Yoshimura, Ken Zame.

PHOTOGRAPHY CREDITS

Lack of space prevents all participants being named alongside their photographs. Nonetheless, the following people's talent and professionalism are gratefully acknowledged.

PAGE 1 Model: Delana Matter (Ford Robert Black – Arizona); Hair/make-up: Miguel Pizzorno; Styling: Debby Dean.

PAGE 3 Model: Angie Ruis; Hair: Gary Novit; Make-up: Maureen Burke; Stylist: Mia Velez.

PAGES 4–5 Models: Lisa Stang and Drew Riker; Hair/make-up: Jules; Stylist: Patrice Goulet.

PAGE 6 Model: Delana Matter; Hair/make-up: Lilian Laureano; Stylist: Wen-Li Ayers; Coordinator: Lilian Laureano.

PAGE 7 Model: Nevrus.

PAGE 10 Model: Matt King.

PAGE 12 Models: Ashli Degenford and Konrad.

PAGE 14 Model: Delana Matter; Hair/make-up: Miguel Pizzorno; Stylist: Debby Dean; Coordinator: Lilian Laureano.

PAGE 17 Model: Kam Heskin; Hair/make-up: Nancy Vela.

PAGE 19 Model: Delana Matter; Hair/make-up: Miguel Pizzorno; Stylist: Debby Dean; Coordinator: Lilian Laureano.

PAGE 21 Model: Charlotte Dodds; Hair: Gary Novit; Make-up: Maureen Burke; Stylist: Debby Dean.

PAGE 27 Models: Kam Heskin and Wil Timmerman; Hair/make-up: Nancy Vela.

PAGES 29–30 Model: Valerie Celis.

PAGE 31 Models: Drew and Derek Riker.

PAGE 32 Model: (middle right) Dawn Gais.

PAGE 33 Model: Delana Matter; Hair/make-up: Miguel Pizzorno; Stylist: Debby Dean; Coordinator: Lilian Laureano.

PAGE 35 (top) Model: Laurie Schumaker; Make-up: Maureen Burke.
(bottom) Model: Stephen T.

PAGES 36–7 Models: Bridget Etzkorn, Tammy Ford, Stephani King, Tiffin, Lisa Stang, Alicia Ogilvy, Liza Cruzat, Marisa Grieco.

PAGES 38–9 Models: Tim Gillespie, Matt King, Michael Anderson, Frank Arends, Derek Riker, Nevrus, Wil Timmerman.

PAGES 40–1 Model: Chris Jensen; Hair/make-up: Miguel Pizzorno; Stylist: Debby Dean; Coordinator: Lilian Laureano.

PAGES 42–3 Diary supplied by Che Sguardo.

PAGE 45 Model's bag: Bridget Etzkorn; Skin care products: Che Sguardo; Stylist: Anne Cole.

PAGE 47 Model's bag: Michael Ramion; Grooming aids: Che Sguardo; Stylist: Anne Cole.

PAGE 48 Model: Delana Matter (Ford Robert Black – Arizona); Hair/make-up: Lilian Laureano; Stylist: Wen-Li Ayers; Coordinator: Lilian Laureano.

PAGES 50–2 Model: Angela Fu; Make-up: Maureen Burke; Hair: Gary Novit; Stylist: Patrice Goulet; Products: M. Burke Maquillage.

PAGE 53 Model: Gian Carlo.

PAGES 54–5 Model: Nevrus; Hair/make-up: Nancy Vela; Grooming aids: Che Sguardo.

PAGE 56 Model: Andrea Chambers; Products: Che Sguardo.

PAGE 57 Model: Angie Ruis; Hair: Gary Novit; Make-up: Nancy Vela; Stylist: Patrice Goulet.

PAGES 58–89 All make-up by Maureen Burke, using M. Burke Maquillage. All hair styling by Gary Novit.

PAGE 58 Model: Charlotte

Dodds; Stylist: Debby Dean.

PAGES 58–65 Model: Charlotte Dodds; Stylist: Patrice Goulet.

PAGE 66 Model: Jahaila Sing; Stylist: Patrice Goulet.

PAGE 67 Models: Gayle Brown, Angela Fu, Angie Ruis; Stylist: Debby Dean.

PAGE 68 Model: Gayle Brown; Stylist: Debby Dean.

PAGE 69 Models: Angela Fu and Angie Ruis; Stylist: Debby Dean.

PAGES 70–1 Beauty products courtesy of Che Sguardo; Stylist: Anne Cole.

PAGES 72–3 Grooming products courtesy of Che Sguardo; Stylist: Anne Cole.

PAGE 75 Model: Marcellas; Make-up: Nancy Vela; Stylist: Debby Dean.

PAGE 76 Model: Angela Fu; Stylist: Patrice Goulet; Hair color: Scott Patrick.

PAGE 77 Model: Kam Heskin; Stylist: Patrice Goulet; Hair color: Scott Patrick.

PAGE 78 Model: Gayle Brown; Stylist: Patrice Goulet; Hair color: Diana Mildice.

PAGE 79 Model: Michael Pater.

PAGE 80 Model: Derek Riker; Make-up: Nancy Vela; Stylist: Debby Dean.

PAGE 81 Models: (top left) Nevrus; (top right) Charlotte Dodds, Drew Riker, Michael Pater, Marcellas; (bottom right) Michael Pater; (bottom right) Marcellas; Make-up: Nancy Vela; Stylist: Debby Dean.

PAGE 82 Model: Jahaila Sing; Stylist: Patrice Goulet; Color technician: Diana Mildice.

PAGE 83 Model: Nevrus; Make-up: Nancy Vela; Color technician: Diana Mildice.

PAGE 85 Model: Jahaila Sing; Make-up: Nancy Vela; Stylist: Patrice Goulet; Hair color: Scott Patrick.

PAGE 86 Model: Angie Ruis; Hairdresser: Gary Novit.

PAGE 87 Models: (top left) Gayle Brown; (top right) Nevrus; (bottom left) Kam Heskin; (bottom right) Derek Riker;

Make-up: Nancy Vela; Stylist: Patrice Goulet.

PAGE 90 Models: Marcellas, Melody Perkins, Nevrus; Hair/make-up: Miguel Pizzorno; Stylist: Debby Dean.

PAGE 93 Models: Stephen, Tiffin, Nevrus, Paul K.

PAGE 95 Model: Tiffin.

PAGE 96 Models: Pilar, Marcellas, Jason Painter.

PAGE 98 Models: Adriana Samudio, Jake Lesada, Ashley Carman, Elaine Opsitnick, Paul K; Hair/make-up: Nick Harris; Stylist: Wen-Li Ayers; Coordinator: Lilian Laureano.

PAGE 101 Model: Jeanette Haskett (David & Lee, Chicago); Hair/make-up: Tina Guzaldo.

PAGE 102-3 Model: Ashley Carman.

PAGE 103 Model: Lisa Stang; Hair/make-up: Nancy Vela; Stylist: Wen-Li Ayers.

PAGE 104 Models: (left): Michelle; (right) Fatima.

PAGE 105 Models: Sharon Scully, Ed Hoban.

PAGE 106–7 Model: Kam Heskin; Hair/make-up: Nancy Vela.

PAGE 108 Models: (left) Drew Riker; (right) Gary Alexander.

PAGE 109 Model: Matt King.

PAGE 110 (left) Originally commissioned by Ogilvy Mather advertising agency; Art director: Barbara Travis; (right) Originally commissioned by Bozell, Jacobs, Kenyon & Eckhardt, Inc.; Client: Contel Telephone Operations; Art director: Kent Ottwell; Model: Irene Best; Hair/make-up: Cindy Adams; Stylist: Diane Pronites.

PAGE 111 Originally commissioned by Frankenberry Laughlin Constible; Art director: Kathy Sherwood; Styling: Francine Gourguechon.

PAGE 112 Originally commissioned by J. Walter Thompson advertising agency; Hand model: Brenda Burns; Swimmer: Lynn Kempton.

PAGE 113 Model: Lisa Stang; Hair/make-up: Jules.

PAGE 115 Model: Brian Zaker; Make-up: Teig; Stylist: Mia Velez.

PAGE 117 Model: Yasmeen.

PAGE 119 Model: Delana Matter; Hair/make-up: Miguel Pizzorno; Stylist: Debby Dean; Coordinator: Lilian Laureano.

PAGE 120 Model: Bethany Winn; Hair/make-up: Lilian Laureano; Stylist: Wen-Li Ayers

PAGE 130 Model: Jahaila Sing; Hair/make-up: Nick Harris; Stylist: Wen-Li Ayers; Coordinator: Lilian Laureano.

PAGE 134 Model: Jahaila Sing; Hair: Gary Novit; Make-up: Maureen Burke; Stylist: Patrice Goulet.

PAGE 135 (top) Model: Nevrus; Color technician: Diana Mildice; (bottom) Model: Derek Riker, with stylists Patrice Goulet and Wen-Li Ayers.

PAGE 138 Model: Andrea Robinson.

PAGES 142-5 Home economist: Lorna Rhodes.

PAGE 146 Model: Lynn Kempton.

PAGE 148 Model: Jahaila Sing; Hair/make-up: Nick Harris;

Stylist: Wen-Li Ayers; Coordinator: Lilian Laureano.

PAGE 149 Models: Lynn Kempton, Jack McIntosh.

PAGES 150-2 Model: Lynn Kempton.

PAGE 153 Model: Polly Martin.

PAGE 154 Model: Monica McGee; Hair/make-up: Ronda Moya; Styling: Debby Dean; Location: Walter E. Smithe showroom; Coordinator: Lilian Laureano.

PAGE 157 Model: Charlotte Dodds.

PAGE 158-60 Calligraphy: Kristel Bosshardt.

PAGE 162 Models: Matt Dabney and Monica McGee; Hair/make-up: Ronda Moya; Stylist: Debby Dean; Location: Act One Studios; Coordinator: Lilian Laureano.

PAGE 171 Model: Charlotte Dodds; Hair/make-up: Jules.

PAGE 174 Model: Michelle Norkett; Hair/make-up: Jules; Stylist: Wen-Li Ayers.

Norman Jean Roy

PUBLISHER'S NOTE
While every effort has been made to ensure the accuracy of these credits, the publishers invite readers to bring any errors or omissions to their attention so that they can be corrected in future editions of the book.

FURTHER READING

Arthur Elgort's Models' Manual, Arthur Elgort (Grand Street Press, New York, 1994).

Catwalk: Inside the World of the Supermodels, Sandra Morris (Universe Publishing, New York, 1995).

International Talent and Modeling Agency Directory, David Vando (Peter Glenn Publishing Co., New York, published yearly).

Model: The Ugly Business of Beautiful Women, Michael Gross (William Morrow, New York, 1995).

Ogilvy on Advertising, David Ogilvy (Vintage Books, Random House, New York, 1985).

Thing of Beauty, Stephen Fried (Pocket Books, New York, 1993).

CHAPTER 8
BIBLIOGRAPHY

Exercise, Education, and Medicine, R. Tait McKenzie (W.B. Saunders Co., Philadelphia and London, 1924).

Human Movement Potential, Lulu E. Sweigard (Harper & Row, New York, 1988).

Kinesiology of the Human Body Under Normal and Pathological Conditions, Dr Arthur Steindler (Charles C. Thomas, 1977).

Lean Bodies, Cliff Sheets (Summit Publishing, Arlington, Texas, USA, 1992).

Nutrition and Diet Therapy, 9th edition, Proudfoot and Robinson (Macmillan, New York, 1946).

Total Body Fitness, Robert Gajda and Dr Richard Dominguez (Warner Books, New York, 1982).

Literature produced by the American Dietetic Association was also extremely useful in devising the menus featured in the chapter.

USEFUL ADDRESSES

The agencies listed below have been established for at least five years and are known to be reputable.

UNITED STATES

ARIZONA
Ford Robert Black – 7525 E. Camelback #200, Scottsdale, AZ 85251 Tel: 602 966 2537

CALIFORNIA
Bordeaux – 616 N. Robertson Blvd., W. Hollywood, CA 90069 Tel: 310 289 2550

City – 123 Townsend #510, San Francisco, CA 94107 Tel: 415 546 3160

Click – 9057 Nemo Street, N. Hollywood, CA 90096 Tel: 310 246 0800

Ford L.A. – 8825 Burton Way, Beverly Hills, CA 90211 Tel: 213 462 7274

LA Models – 8335 Sunset Blvd, Los Angeles, CA 90069 Tel: 213 656 9572

Look – 166 Geary Street, San Francisco, CA 94108 Tel: 415 781 2822

Next – 662 N. Robertson Blvd., W. Hollywood, CA 90069 Tel: 310 358 0100

Stars – 777 Davis Street, San Francisco, CA 94111 Tel: 415 421 6272

United-Prima – 933 North LaBrea Ave, Los Angeles, CA 90038 Tel: 213 882 6900

Wilhelmina West – 8383 Wilshire Blvd., Beverly Hills, CA 90211 Tel: 213 655 0909

COLORADO
Donna Baldwin – 50 S. Steele Street, Denver CO 80209 Tel: 303 320 0067

Maximum – 3900 E. Mexico Ave., Denver, CO 80210 Tel: 303 691 2344

Siegel Represents – 1539 Platte Street #205, Denver, CO 80202 Tel: 303 433 0660

FLORIDA
Alexa – 4100 W. Kennedy, Tampa, FL 33609 Tel: 813 289 8020

Cassandra & Bailey – 513 W. Colonial Dr., Orlando, FL 32804 Tel: 407 423 7872

Click – 161 Ocean Drive, Miami Beach, FL 33139 Tel: 305 674 9900

Coloures – 1655 Drexel, Miami Beach, FL 33139 Tel: 305 531 2700

Ford – 826 Ocean Drive, Miami Beach, FL 33139 Tel: 305 534 7200

Irene Marie – 728 Ocean Drive, Miami Beach, FL 33139 Tel: 305 672 2929

Mens Board – 1688 Meridian #1025, Miami Beach, FL 33135 Tel: 305 531 1610

Michelle Pommier – 81 Washington Ave., Miami Beach, FL 33139 Tel: 305 674 7206

MMG – 804 Ocean Drive, Miami Beach, FL 33139 Tel: 305 672 8300

Next – 209 Ninth Street, Miami, FL 33139 Tel: 305 531 5100

Page Parkes – 763 Collins, Miami Beach, FL 33139 Tel: 305 672 4869

GEORGIA
Arlene Wilson – 887 W. Marietta Street, N.W. #101, Atlanta, GA 30318 Tel: 404 876 8555

L'Agence – 5901 C. Peachtree Dunwoody Road N.E., Atlanta, GA 30328 Tel: 404 396 9015

Michelle Pommier – 1 Baltimore Place #360, Atlanta, GA 30308 Tel: 404 815 5888

HAWAII
Central Island Agency – 41-846 Laumilo Street, Waimanalo, HI 96795 Tel: 808 259 7914

ILLINOIS
Aria – 1017 West Washington #2A, Chicago, IL 60607 Tel: 312 243 9400

MASSACHUSETTS
The Models Group – 374 Congress Street #305, Boston, MA 02210 Tel: 617 426 4711

NEW YORK
American – 155 Spring Street, New York, NY 10012 Tel: 212 941 5858

Boss – 1 Ganesvoort Street, New York, NY 10014

Tel: 212 242 2444

Click – 881 Seventh Avenue, New York NY 10019 Tel: 212 315 2200

Elite – 111 East 22nd Street, New York, NY 10010 Tel: 212 529 9800

Ford – 3142 Green Street, New York, NY 10012 Tel: 212 966 3565

IMG – 170 Fifth Ave., New York, NY 10010 Tel: 212 627 0400

Next – 23 Watts, New York, NY 10013 Tel: 212 925 5100

Wilhelmina – 300 Park Ave. S., New York, NY 10010 Tel: 212 473 0700

Zoli – 3 West 18th Street, New York, NY 10011 Tel: 212 242 5959

TEXAS
Campbell Agency – 3906 Lemmon Ave. #200, Dallas TX 75219. Tel: 214 522 8991

Kim Dawson – 1643 Apparel Mart, PO Box 585060, Dallas, TX 75258 Tel: 214 638 2414

Page Parkes – 3303 Lee Parkway, Dallas, TX 75219 Tel: 214 526 4434

CANADA
Charles Stuart – 1008 Homer Street, Vancouver, BC V6B 2X1 Tel: 604 683 4080

Folio – 295 de la Commune Ouest, Montreal, QB H2Y 2E1 Tel: 514 288 8080

Ford – 3 Sultan Street, Toronto, ONT M5S 1L6 Tel: 416 962 6500

Giovanni – 13 Clarence Square, Toronto, ONT M5V 1H1 Tel: 416 597 1993

Montage– 3451 St. Laurent, Montreal, QB H2X 2T6 Tel: 514 284 4901

Sherrida – 110 Scollard Street, Toronto, ONT M5R 1G2 Tel: 416 928 2323

OVERSEAS AGENCIES

The following list is a selection of established agencies with whom you are likely to come into contact once your modeling career has taken off. More detailed information about some of these markets is given in Chapter 6.

AUSTRALIA

Camerons – Edgecliffe Court, 2 McLean Street, Edgecliffe NSW 2027 Tel: 61 2 362 0100

Chadwicks – 32A Oxford Street, Darlinghurst, Sydney NSW 2010 Tel: 61 2 332 4177

Chic – 155 New South Head Road, Edgecliffe, NSW 2027 Tel: 61 2 328 6900

F.R.M. – 9 Coolullah Avenue, South Yarra, Melbourne 3141 Tel: 61 3 9827 0943

Gordon Charles – 49 Bay Street, Double Bay, NSW 2028 Tel: 61 2 327 8722

Priscilla's – 185 Elizabeth Street, Sydney 2000 Tel: 61 2 261 1512

Vivien's – 43 Bay Street, Double Bay NSW 2028 Tel: 61 2 326 2700

AUSTRIA

Flair – Nusswaldgasse 19, A-1190 Vienna Tel: 43 1 369 8436

Next – Werdertorgasse 12, 1010 Vienna Tel: 43 1 535 9669

Tausendassa – Heitzinger Haupstrasse 28, 1130 Vienna Tel: 43 1 878 770

Wiener Models – Rudolfsplatz 10/4, 1010 Vienna Tel: 43 1 533 2277

DENMARK

Scandinavian Models – 10 Magstraede, DK 1204, Copenhagen K Tel: 45 33 93 24 24

Unique – NY Ostergade 3, DK 1101, Copenhagen K Tel: 45 33 12 00 55

ENGLAND

Laraine Ashton – 13–16 Jacob's Well Mews, London W1H 5PD Tel: 71-486 8021

Bookings – 6 Pembridge Studios, 27a Pembridge Villas, London W11 3EP

Tel: 71-221 2603

Boss – 7 Berners Mews, London W1P 3DG Tel: 71-580 2444

Elite Premier – Elite House, 40–42 Parker Street, London WC2B 5PH Tel: 71-333 0888

IMG – 13–16 Jacob's Well Mews, London W1H 5PD Tel: 71-486 8011

Matthews & Powell – 104–112 Marylebone Lane, London W1M 5FU Tel: 71-224 0560

Models One – Omega House, 471–473 Kings Road, London SW10 0LU Tel: 71-351 6033

Nevs – 36 Walpole Street, London SW3 4QS Tel: 71-730 9138

Profile – 12–13 Henrietta Street, London WC2E 8LH Tel: 71-836 5282

Select – 43 King Street, London WC2E 8RJ Tel: 71-470 5200

Storm – 5 Jubilee Place, London SW3 3TD Tel: 71-376 7764

Two Management – 11 Garrick Street, London WC2 9AR Tel: 71-836 4501

Ugly – 256 Edgware Road, London W2 1DS Tel: 71-402 5564

FINLAND

Paparazzi – Salomonkatu 17 8 30, 00100 Helsinki Tel: 358 0 694 5200

FRANCE

Bananas Mambo – 217 rue du Faubourg Saint-Honoré 75008 Paris Tel: 33 1 42 89 42 09

City – 21 rue Jean Mermoz, 75008 Paris Tel: 33 1 43 59 54 95

Company – 26 rue de la Tremoille, 75008 Paris Tel: 33 1 53 67 77 00

Elite – 8 bis rue Lecuirot, 75014 Paris Tel: 33 1 40 44 32 22

FAM – 13 rue de Washington, 75008 Paris Tel: 33 1 45 62 58 35

Ford – 29 rue Danielle Casanova, 75001 Paris Tel: 33 1 40 20 98 40

IMG – 2 rue du Frenoy, 75116 Paris Tel: 33 1 45 03 85 00

Karin – 9 avenue Hoche, 75008 Paris Tel: 33 1 45 63 08 23

Marilyn Gautier– 4 rue de la Paix, 75002 Paris Tel: 33 1 53 29 53 53

Success – 64 rue Rambuteau, 75003 Paris Tel: 33 1 42 78 89 89

Viva! – 15 rue Duphot, 75001 Paris Tel: 33 1 44 55 12 60

GERMANY

Body & Soul – Heinrich Barth Strasse 21, 20146 Hamburg Tel: 49 40 4120 91

E-Models – Cornelius Strasse 71, 40215 Dusseldorf Tel: 49 21 1386 100

Harry's – Virchow Strasse 2, 80805 Munich Tel: 49 89 360 0000

Louisa – Ebersberger Strasse 9, 81679 Munich Tel: 49 89 921096 20

Mega – Wexstrasse 26, 20355 Hamburg Tel: 49 40 3430 09

Model Team – Schluterstrasse 60, 20146 Hamburg Tel: 49 40 4141037

Munich Models – Karl Theodorestrasse 18A, 80803 Munich Tel: 49 89 341336

Nova – Antonienstrasse 3, 80802 Munich Tel: 49 89 347027

Okay – Rödingsmarkt 52, 20459 Hamburg Tel: 49 40 378500-0

Promod – Barmbekerstrasse 136, 22299 Hamburg Tel: 49 40 4710000

Talents – Muhlenkamp 31, 22303 Hamburg Tel: 49 40 271047

GREECE

Ace – 9 Irodotou Street, 10674 Athens Tel: 30 1 725 8531

Action – Patriarchou Ioakim 11, 10675 Athens Tel: 30 1 721 10 75

Agence S.A. – 15 Karneadou Street, 10675 Athens Tel: 30 1 729 2611

Fashion Cult – 5 Yperidou Street, 10558 Athens

Tel: 30 1 322 00 24

HOLLAND

De Boekers – Herengracht 407 1017 BP Amsterdam Tel: 31 20 627 2766

Corine's – Prinsengracht 678, 1017 KX Amsterdam Tel: 31 20 622 6755

Elite – Keizersgracht 448, 1016 GD Amsterdam Tel: 31 20 627 9929

Name – Herengracht 16, 1015 BK Amsterdam Tel: 31 20 638 1217

Ulla – Weteringschans 18, 1017 SG Amsterdam Tel: 31 20 626 3676

IRELAND

The Agency – 38 Clarendon Street, Dublin 2 Tel: 1 679 4277

Morgan Brand – 13 Herbert Place, Dublin 2 Tel: 1 676 6625

ITALY

Beatrice – Via Vincenzo Monti 47, 20123 Milan Tel: 39 1 2 4692 599

Eye For I – Via Aurelio Saffi 29, 20123 Milan Tel: 39 1 2 4801 2877

Fashion – Via Monte Rosa 80 20149 Milan Tel: 39 1 2 4808 6222

Italy – Via Seprio 2, 20149 Milan Tel: 39 1 2 4801 2828

Joy – Via San Vittore 40, 20123 Milan Tel: 39 1 2 4800 2776

Jump – Via Settembrini 17, 20124 Milan Tel: 39 1 2 6707 0523

Look Now – Via Alberto Giussano 16, 20145 Milan Tel: 39 1 2 4802 0126

Model Plan – Via Revere 8, 20123 Milan Tel: 39 1 2 4800 2712

Riccardo Gay –Via Revere 8, 20123 Milan Tel: 39 1 2 4800 2713

Why Not – Via Gioberti 2, 20123 Milan Tel: 39 1 2 4818 341

JAPAN

Agence Presse – 503 Aoyama Heights, 5-10-5 Minami Aoyama, Minato-Ku,

Cinq Deux Un – 9-6-28 Akasaka, Minato-Ku Tokyo 107 Tel: 81 3 3402 8445

Elite Folio – 3F, 3-16-15 Roppongi, Minato-Ku, Tokyo 106 Tel: 81 3 3587 0200

Kirara – Kitaya Mansion 203, 1-7-9 Jinnan, Shibuya-Ku, Tokyo 150 Tel: 81 3 3461 5540

Select/Eve –1-2-2-200 Umeda, Kita-Ku, Osaka 530 Tel: 81 6 344 6346

Yo – A La Croce 302, 5-4-24 Minamiaoyama, Minato-Ku, Tokyo 107 Tel: 81 3 546 0260

Yoshie Inc. – #302 K's Apt., 4-30-22 Taishido, Setagaya-Ku, Tokyo 107 Tel: 81 3 5481 2224

Zem – Wakasugi Building 9F, 2-3-13 Sonezaki Shinchi, Kita-Ku, Osaka 530 Tel: 81 6 341 5252

SCOTLAND
Model Team Scotland – 180 Hope Street, Glasgow G2 2UE Tel: 41-332 1915

SOUTH AFRICA
Heads – 79 Oxford Road, Saxonworld, Johannesburg 2196 Tel: 27 11 442 6020

Max – 9 Union Street Gardens, Cape Town 8000 Tel: 27 21 240 108

Model Company – 1 Glenhove Road, Rosebank, Johannesburg 2196 Tel: 21 11 788 0323

Outlaws – 11 Wessels Road, Greenpoint, Cape Town 8001 Tel: 27 21 439 3999

SPAIN
Francina – General Mitre 170, 08006 Barcelona Tel: 34 3 212 5624

La Agencia – Av. Diagonal 449, 08036 Barcelona Tel: 34 3 444 3000

Natasha's – Av. Diagonal 469, 08036 Barcelona Tel: 34 3 405 3435

New Group – Alcala 87, 28009 Madrid Tel: 34 1 431 3011

PH One – Calle Diego de Leon 51, 28006 Madrid Tel: 34 1 564 2929

Stars – Sagasta 4, 28004 Madrid Tel: 34 1 521 1111

Traffic – Calle Beethoven 15, 08021 Barcelona Tel: 34 3 414 1404

SWEDEN
Mika's – Ragvaldsgatan 14 S-118 46 Stockholm Tel: 46 8 641 0801

Stockholmsgruppen – 57 Mosebacke Torg 4, 116 46 Stockholm Tel: 46 8 644 8300

SWITZERLAND
Charlotte Fischer – Markusstrasse 20, CH–8006 Zurich Tel: 41 1 363 1958

Model Team – Hegibach Strasse 68, 8032 Zurich Tel: 41 1 353 357

Option – Stussi Strasse 83, 8057 Zurich Tel: 41 1 363 6020

PMS – Rieterstrasse 21, CH-8002 Zurich Tel: 41 1 202 3744

Time – Spitalgasse 4, 8001 Zurich Tel: 41 1 261 6040

Vogue – Utoquai 31, 8008 Zurich Tel: 41 1 261 0422

Modeling Information

from

Aria Model & Talent Management Ltd.

1.900 988 8888

$3.00/minute – average 5-8 minutes a call

Monday – Friday 10:00 a.m. – 4:00 p.m. Central Standard Time

Must be 18 years of age

Aria Model & Talent Management Ltd. Chicago, Illinois

Customer Service 312 243 9400

INDEX